What Hap

Happened

a work of friction by   Neumann

Happenings

DEDICATED ACKNOWLEDGMENTS

To everyone who has influenced, inspired, and impacted my life...you
should know that the only reason I can write about
what had happened is because of you.

For reasons that are much more better than worse, you are all the
reasons why I am the way that I am, and for that I can only say,

Thank You

WHAT THE...

What the hell.

It's not so much a question as it is an overall observation.

My life as a teacher.

What (*pause*) the (*longer pause*) hell.

That's what I've been asking myself every single school day for the past 5 years. What the hell am I doing? What the hell am I supposed to be doing? What the hell am I teaching? Hell, am I teaching? What the hell are my students learning? What the hell are they doing? What the hell can I do to prepare these kids for life after public school?

What the hell am I doing with my life?

Questions.

Not so very long ago, I decided there was a need to clarify my interpretations....ya know, narrow the scope of my hellish colloquial approximations. So, for awhile now I've been writing about my observational experiences as a high school english teacher.

Don't worry, the 'e' in english has been left lowercase for a reason.

If you're reading this book, I am no longer an english teacher.

If you finish this book, you will know why.

But before we really get going, you should know I've never been much of a troublemaker.

Even though high school is the perfect breeding ground for the kind of arrested development that enraptures most adolescent males, I don't know that I ever quite fit the bill.

The first time I went to high school, I stayed off the administrative radar. At the close of my senior year, I'd never been written up.

Written up = student behaves poorly in school and is consequently reprimanded by administrative personnel via written...whatever.

Flash forward to the end of my first day as a high school english teacher. Bell rings, students evacuate, and wadded up pieces of notebook paper ornament the trashcan by my door like presents under a Christmas tree. The left-to-right clatter of wedge heels echo off the industrial tile floor as I'm about to sit down for the first time in hours. A 20 year veteran, the one in control of the previously mentioned wedges, from across the hall shuffles over to my door to ask me if I had to write any referrals on my first day. Before I can even formulate a proper reply, she interrupts me with another question.

"Sweetie, do you even know where the referral forms are?"

Me = No.

I am freshman...again. My colleague from across the way politely but knowingly escorts me to the departmental office where a surplus of referral forms decorated in perforated edges and carbon triplicate reside. By the time I'm back in my classroom I have a stack of referral forms "just in case."

Ms. Jones shuffles back across the hallway in the finely crafted wedges she bought from some sort of indigenous people in a part of the world I've never heard of. I thank her in a repetitive fashion, shut the door to Room 300 and sit down for the first time since 6:30 AM.

It's 4:00 PM.

I am exhaustion.

Staring blankly at the stack of referral forms, I realize there is, in fact, someone I need to write up. Myself.

"Please describe, in full, the infraction."

Sucking at life.

"Could you be a bit more specific?"

Surely...from1997 to 2001, I attended high school in a middle to upper middle socioeconomic school district. I was privileged and took it for granted. I lacked motivation, social skills, and an open mind. I was angry, distant, and so utterly immersed in self pity and self loathing I was unable to realize how fortunate I was. More to the point, I was clueless. For 4 years, I was a drain on my community.

"Recommended disciplinary action:"

4 years community service. That is to say, 4 years public service. And in consideration of accrued interest, it is recommended that the offender also serve one additional year. So, in total, that'll be 5 years Neumann. This'll provide you with a rather unique opportunity to experience high school from a perspective that is entirely different from that of your previous attempt.

5 years as a high school english teacher in an environment that, at least initially, makes the offender (Neumann) feel more than uncomfortable.

The first time I got written up, I wrote myself up.

At the start of this project, I've served 3.5 years of my debt to society. It is my hope that writing about, and in reference to, the last 18 months proves to be...educational if nothing else.

So from here on out, I just thought you should know the stories contained within these pages are intended for the persons or entities interested in reading them and may contain confidential, proprietary, and/or extremely sarcastic material.

Any review, retransmission, dissemination or other use of, or taking of any action in reliance upon these stories by persons or entities other than the intended recipients is seriously frowned upon...dude.

Away we go.

BUTTON DIRECTIVES

"The white call button in your classroom is to be used for emergencies only."

I never use my call button...well, there was that one time a female student went into labor during class, but, I mean, that was an emergency. I didn't know what to do.

"An emergency may be an actual fight that occurs while class is in session, or even a student who has become so disorderly that you are no longer able to control your classroom. If either of those things should happen, it is acceptable to push the call button."

This is the sound of protocol. A middle-aged administrator stands in front of a theater stage and projects his booming voice to the faculty and staff without microphone. No one sits in the front rows; unless he or she is an administrator.

Teachers are like students; they don't want to sit in the front of the room anymore than they want someone telling them how to run their classroom. No one wants to sit in the front. The front is for suck-ups. The front is for people with something to say.

"Now substitute teachers are a whole different story. They don't know how to handle our students. Substitutes can and will push the call button at any time, for any reason, no matter what."

The auditorium laughs. Glancing over at the illuminated agenda on the transportable projector screen, I wonder how much I'm actually going to get done today.

Teacher Workday

day before Spring semester begins

Proceedings...

8:30-9:20 am (Faculty Meeting in Theater)

Greetings from the new Assistant Superintendent.

From all I can tell, the average permanence of most educational figures above the noble title of "teacher" seems to be 3-5 years. That is to say, their positions seem to be of a transient nature at best.

The previous Assistant Superintendent left one indelible memory burning on the frayed edges of my idealistic synapses about 2.5 years ago. He was yammering on to us teacher folk about textbooks. What can be learned from textbooks and what can't be learned from textbooks. Long story short, he told us that even if we taught our students everything contained in our respective anthologies, we'd only be teaching our students 40% of what they really need to know.

I stopped using textbooks the next day. Haven't used them since.

Spring semester protocols, updates, adjustments.

Actually known as: To Push or not To Push, when to use your call button.

9:30am- 12:00pm (Time to Work in "your" classroom)

I found this one out the hard way. Working in your classroom does not mean you should spend a ridiculous amount of time decorating, painting, and/or making the classroom a fuzzy little welcoming center that fosters the development of your students in a progressive yet structured way.

An assumption on my part, and an incorrect one at that. However, if you have time to do all of that congenial atmospheric nurturing nature crap, by all means, go for it.

Time to work in your classroom means:

This is not "your" classroom. The county you work for owns the classroom you teach in. So, bottom line, don't paint the walls. It's like you're renting the place. Whatever white walls you paint over now, you will just have to paint white again whenever, heaven forbid, you are no longer in "your" classroom.

12:00pm-1:00pm (Lunch on your own)

Eating lunch only takes 10 minutes.

1:00pm-2:45pm (English Department Meeting)

Students aren't supposed to use their cell phones in school. As role models, and I guess just out of a general respect for one another and overall professionalism, teachers are not supposed to use their cell phones during school hours either.

Right.

2:45pm-4:00pm (Time to work in your classroom)

Students return tomorrow. Check my mailbox on the way out. New class rosters, compilations of student identification numbers, schedule verification forms, and corresponding transcripts rest quietly in the black metal drawer. It's like a minnie coffin.

Organized chaos. There isn't a call button in the mailroom.

NUMBER WITH NO NAME

You have one saved message.

Saved message...

(static) + Happy New Year!...Neumannator, what's happenin man. Uh, hope you had a nice little Christmas with your wife. Tell Ma...uh...crap...starts with a M...Mara! Heelll yea. Tell Mara I said hello and uh Merry Christmas...kinda past already I'm kinda late. Just thinking...uh Happy New Year buddy! Hope to see ya in yur classroom bright and early whatever morning we get back. I don't even know, damn...when do we get back? Alright, see ya Neumannator...+ (static)

*...To replay message press **1**.*

*To delete press **7**.*

*To save press **9**.*

*For more options press **6**.*

Nine.

Andre called after I fell asleep. We're talking like, out cold, non-responsive, comatose through the night without moving a muscle type sleep. Welcome to the standard school night. Starting the day at 4AM, you begin to question the boundaries of reality when the clock reads 11:30PM.

I didn't even realize I had a missed call until 7:15 this morning. About to walk out the door, kiss Mara goodbye, gathering all my stuff and what not, and I saw that little cassette reel thing signifying the pending voice message.

Andre calls fairly often; usually about random stuff.

For example, shortly after the floods this past fall = ring ring + caller ID:

Neumann = Hey Man.

Andre = Neumann...Six Flags is under water....like, uh...that big white roller coaster...Scream Machine or whatever the hell it's called, half of it's under water...what are you up to?

Andre was a student of mine about a year and a half ago. He stops by the classroom regularly, for a variety of reasons, at varying times throughout the day. One, he likes the music on my iPOD. Two, I let him use "my" classroom as a locker/closet. Three, I give him a ride home every once and awhile because he lives out of district (long story). And four, we're friends.

By the time I actually get in my car it's 7:21AM.

I should tell Andre that Mara's working for an architectural firm in Atlanta now. He'll get a kick out of that.

Ignition turn. No start. Come on Lucile...ignition turn...Start! There we go. iPOD scroll + Ben Harper + Relentless 7 = Number With No Name

The semester may officially begin.

D-BAG

I pledge allegiance, to the flag, of the United States of A**NEUMANN**!!

I'm closing the door to Room 300 with my left hand. The intercom speaks of pledging compliance. Right hand over the heart. Momentum moving me inward to Room 300 with the swinging of door hinges. The words, "of America," are automatic but someone interrupts me this morning.

NEUMANN!! Hey! Wait! Neumann, no! Hold the door!

8:25AM is the official start of the academic school day.

8:25AM means homeroom teachers should shut their doors, recite the pledge, observe a moment of silence, and most importantly, make sure all students are where they need to be....theoretically, this means students should be in classrooms; not hallways.

Andre was in the hallway at 8:25AM. Well actually, Andre was shouting down the hallway in my general direction as neighboring teachers were shutting their classroom doors. Some teachers paused, stared at the ruckus, then at me, then at the ruckus...sprinkle in a little silent awkwardness and we're good to go.

Thanks Neumann.

(Insert head nod and barely audible "no problem")

I shut the door to Room 300. One student stands attentive during the pledge. The rest sit indifferently, directing their attention elsewhere, on different devices, and in different dispositions.

With liberty and justice for all.

Neumann...oh hey I need one of those (points at a schedule verification bla bla bla) **uh, Neumann...what'd I wanna say...could you walk into a Title & Loan with only the title and still get the loan? Like, do you think I'd need to have the car too or could I just show em the title?**

Please observe a moment of quiet reflection. Thank you intercom.

Homeroom ends. Students are to report to 1st Block. Students are allotted 7 minutes to change classes. Teachers are asked to stand outside their classroom doors during the 7 minute flux to help facilitate students from one area to the next, enforce school policies relating to dress code and electronic devices, prevent/report/stop fights from happening, and so on and so forth.

Very few teachers stand outside their doorways during class changes on a regular basis.

I stand outside my door during every class change. My students know it too.

They're not allowed to stand in my spot outside my door. It's not like a rule or anything, but I'll just be like, "dude! you're in my spot," and that's it.

So yeah, standing. Time = 8:26AM. Student from last semester walks up to me at my spot outside my door and asks:

"Hey Mr. Neumann. (short pause) Do you (short pause) remember my friend (short pause) Travis?"

Me = Ummm, n(delayed)o. Can't say that I do man, but...I'm not really that good with names. I might know him if I saw him.

Jake = Oh (longer pause) well....do uh, can you come here for second?

Me = Yeah sure, does you're friend have a class up here or something?

Jake = Yeah, uh, he's right down here. (2 doors down on right)

Me = Alright, cool.

We walk.

Jake = (standing outside the door but pointing his index finger inward) See that kid wearing the black hat with the flaps?

Me = Yep.

Meanwhile, kid (otherwise known as Travis) with black hat turns his head to see us seeing him. He quickly takes off his hat and turns his head back, eyes away from us, not wanting to make visual contact.

Jake and Travis are not friends.

Jake = Yeah (clears his throat). He tried to give himself a haircut over break. Look at the back. Doesn't he look like a fucking d-bag?

Jake could easily be written into **Superbad**.

Me = (surprised expression...ya know, eyes open wider. Mouth remains closed. Eyebrows raise) Seriously Jake!? That's what you brought me down here for? He does not look like a f...(almost slipped). He looks fine. (I turn to the kid) You look fine. Don't listen to Jake. He has filter problems. (I look back at Jake). Come on man! (I give him a friendly shove in the opposite direction and go back to my door spot. You never know when an administrator is gonna show up.)

Sometimes I forget how mean we were in high school.

I never forget how inappropriate we were.

Bells about to ring. Be positive...I think this to myself.

30 seconds.

Be patient.

Bite my lip to stay awake.

Ring Ring.

Beginith Round One.

ICEBREAKER

Scoot Ova Nigga.

This one does it for me. I've told a few people the condensed version–ya know, my 30 second elevator pitch, the long and short of it–but here's what actually happened.

New Student A = *Scoot Ova Nigga.*

New Student B = **NO.**

New Student A = *Betta watch how you talkin ta me!*

New Student B = **I ain't gotta watch shit!**

New Student A = *What!...you wanna do somethin bout it!?!*

New Student B = **Hell Yeah!**

Commence stupidity.

In a real teacher story, if there's a moral at all, it's like a bloodstain on your shirt sleeve. You can't just wash it out. You can't extract the meaning without bleaching some of the original material. Doesn't matter if it's color safe or not. And in the end, there's nothing much to say about a real teacher story, except maybe "Oh."

Real teacher stories do not simplify.

They do not entertain abstraction or analysis.

For example: Teaching is hell. As an ethical affirmation the old saying seems all well and good, and yet because it abstracts, because it simplifies, I can't believe it with my heart. Nothing beats inside.

Bottom line...it comes down to gut instinct. A real teacher story, if candidly told, makes the heart believe.

But anyway, we crossed a campus that's been under construction since May and meandered towards my classroom (Room 300). It was the first day of the new semester. 4th block...last class of the day. 20 minutes into the period, I unlock my door and welcome students back into class. They were all reestablishing their seats, politely compliant, and then I was in the middle of the most out-of-control situation I've experienced to date. The testosterone was thick, it took nearly an hour to get my nerves back.

Later, at home that night, I told Mara what had happened. What I was doing earlier that afternoon I don't know–no rhyme or reason-but I got in between two boys and tried to stop something bad from happening and may have caused more harm than good. After dinner I went over to the couch and passed out.

New Student A = Scoot Ova Nigga.

New Student B = NO.

New Student A = Betta watch how you talkin ta me!

New Student B = I ain't gotta watch shit!

New Student A = What!...you wanna do somethin bout it!?!

New Student B = Hell Yeah!

Believe it or not, this whole thing started over a chair.

Like, plenty of seats available in class, but one boy wanted another boy's chair...so yeah, away we go. I overhear what's being said, basic shit talking 101, but am not overly concerned until both boys stand-up and square off. I step in the middle, arms raised in an attempt to keep one boy away from the other. It's the first day of classes after all...surely there won't be a fight; especially in my class.

Naive assumptions.

Verbal abuse ensues while the general population remains seated and attentive. Each boy begins to jockey back and forth. I couldn't tell you who swung first. I'm guessing it was the boy who instigated the whole thing because he was the first one I had to restrain.

Most fights I've been in...or rather, the majority of fights I've had to breakup, as soon as I'm able to contain one boy, the fight usually ends. Either the other "fighter" is detained by someone else, or he's just not stupid enough to go after the recently constrained.

I suppose there's a first time for everything.

I couldn't tell you who swung first. The momentum of the situation pushed us forward, towards the front of class. I had the instigator in some form of a headlock but could feel him trying to go against the grain, towards the other boy. And as for that other boy, well, he was behind me the whole time, waiting for the perfect opportunity to strike. The three of us are falling into desks...into other students...and as we are about to fall onto a young lady and her desk, she gets up and I throw the instigator on top of the desk hoping that one of the other boys in class will do me the most tremendous of favors, and hold him down.

Immediately, I turn around and begin pushing the other boy away from the instigator...trying desperately to get him towards the classroom door and out into the hallway.

T'was not to be.

No one tried to contain the instigator, and as I glance out the corner of my eye I notice him making his way, however rapidly, towards myself and the boy I'm trying to move into the hallway. It's a clear path towards the both of us with no one person, nor a single piece of classroom furniture, to block his path. Once again, I turn to intercept the instigator and push him around the both of us and into a table where some students are still sitting...near the very door I'm wanting one of them to exit. He falls onto the table and yet again, I feel the other boy right behind me and somehow manage to body block him into the bookcase adjacent to the classroom door. He was low, as if he'd just come out of a three-point-stance, so when I blocked him from getting to the other instigator his head caught the corner of the book shelf so as to provide a dull thump for all to hear.

I've been in the middle of many a fight, both school related and non-school related, but this is the only one I ever thought, "Shit Ryan, you're gonna get yourself laid out by one of these kids."

It was at that point that some other boys finally came to the rescue. They got the instigator wrapped up as I opened the classroom door, pushed the bookcase boy out, told him to "Stay right there, " and closed the door. The instigator was seated...in the very seat he wanted before this whole thing began, mumbling and endless amount of incoherent profanity meant for the other boy.

Heart in throat, I unfastened the collar to my white button-down shirt, loosened my tie, removed said tie and threw it down to the ground...in the corner between the bookcase and the classroom door, untucked my shirt, and tried to forget the infinite amount of debilitating things I wanted to do to this kid. The chair he was sitting in would be enough. No other props needed.

Several minutes passed before I couldn't hear every beat of my heart.

The rest of the class sat in a silence that was deafening. For a time no one spoke. We had all just witnessed something essential, something brand new and profound, a piece of the semester so startling there was not yet a name for it.

Somebody tapped the instigator on the shoulder.

He was still shit talking, though just barely audible, towards the floor.

"Amazing," I said. "You're still talking. Why are you still talking?"

I glare at him, unblinking, then avert my eyes and open the door to check on the whereabouts of the other fighter. He was standing against a locker, talking to himself.

Close the door without saying so much as a word. Still trying to compose myself. The white call button is not close, and right now, I'm the only discernible object between further transgressions.

I pick up my black and blue stripped tie. Wrap it around the knuckles on my right hand, unravel it, and drop it on the table where, only minutes before, the instigator fell.

Tried asking the student who sat closest to the white call button to press it for me, only the words didn't come out at first. Cleared my throat and tried again.

"Jared, could you press the white call button (I point), please."

Jared, a student I've known for a number of years at this point, obliges my request and pushes the button. Afterward, we all sat waiting for the front office to buzz back but no one ever did.

For thirty minutes we all sat there respectfully. Even sent a girl down the hallway about 15 minutes in, to an administrator's office, so as to inform her of our predicament and request help but apparently the administration was busy...when the student came back from the administrative office down the hall the message was, "She (administrator) said she can't come right now. She's busy."

"Amazing," I kept thinking. "Never been involved in anything like this before."

Informed the class that until our little situation was resolved, I was going to be standing right where I was...in front of the classroom door and between the two gentlemen who decided to reinvent the rules of Musical Chairs.

The instigator, who, now having secured his seat for several minutes, raised his head. "What, you think I'm gonna try and go out there?"

Me = I don't know what you're going to do. I don't know you, remember. This is the first day of class.

Instigator = I'm good. I mean, I'm staying right here...not gonna go anywhere.

Me = That's great. So happy to hear that you're good. Makes my day.

How do you simplify?

Teaching is hell, but that's not the half of it, because teaching is also a mystery and mind-numbing and exciting and courage and discovery and decency and shame and despair and longing and confining and...defining. Teaching is malicious; teaching is fun. Teaching is thrilling; teaching is destructive. Teaching has made me a man; teaching has killed me.

The old adages are contradictory. It can be debated, for example, that teaching where I teach, and not taking it upon myself to seek out other forms of employment, is bizarre. But in all honesty, teaching where I teach is also balance. For all its stress, I can't help but gape at the awful majesty of this occupation. I stare out in the far corner of the parking lot some mornings and watch the campus come to life. I sit in my classroom long after the school day has ended, at times expressionless to both the day that has transpired and the day that has yet to come. I begin to admire the fluid madness of initiatives on the up-and-up, the harmonies of noise and scape and acronyms, the great walls of data streaming down from conference rooms, the highlighted timelines, the white copy paper, the reddish-orange Georgia clay, the angry red stares. It's not pretty, exactly. It's astonishing. If fills the mind...like, it almost commands me. I hate it, yes, but my eyes can't seem to look away. Like oil spilling into the ocean, like a corpse consumed by cancer, any fight or school-wide lockdown has the addictive draw of a bystander's indifference–a commanding, relentless fixation–and a real teacher story will expose the truth about this. And what I've come to find at the beginning of my career is simple...the truth is ugly.

So, after 30 minutes of no help, I send a text message to my department chair.

Me = So umm, just had a fight in class with no administrative response. If you happen to see any (administrators) could you send them my way :)

Department Chair = Oh shit I will send one right away.

Me = Thanks :)

Five minutes later an administrator shows up and escorts the two young men to her office. Once there, they write their statements and I don't see them for the rest of the day. However, before walking the two boys down to her office, she asks me to write a referral, ya know, regarding what had happened, as soon as possible. I close my door and check my phone one more time.

1 New Text Message

Department Chair = Are you okay?

ice-break-er

[ahys-brey-ker]

-noun

1. nautical...a ship specially built for breaking navigable passages through ice.

2. an opening remark, action, etc., designed to ease tension or formality:

A mild joke can be a good icebreaker.

The standard, "Hello, my name is so and so. I am from so and so. I like to do so and so and so and so."

Fighting in class can be a good icebreaker.

3. a tool or machine for chopping ice into small pieces.

1 New Text Message

Department Chair = Are you okay?

Good question. Valid question. Am I okay?

As the silence becomes nearly insurmountable, one girl, sitting in the very front of the room, raises her hand in bold desperation. No time to think about the textual question.

"Are weeee going...to have...like, an icebreaker or something?"

Me = Haha, ummm, well...I think we just had one.

A few students laugh. Others turn to look at her with this, "Did you really just ask that question?"...expression.

Girl = Oh, right, well then what are we supposed to be doing?

Me = I'm pretty sure that before all this happened, I asked you to begin writing a response to the two questions (1 point) I have on the screen up there. What is your favorite spot/place at this high school?...and what is the relationship between this place and you?...300 written words per question...due tomorrow, yes?

Girl = Ohhhh...K...well then I'll just beee...writing then, right.

Me = Well, I mean, if you're having trouble with that first one (although everyone in class is already listening to our conversation I begin looking around the room to acknowledge other no name faces) you could try the other end of the spectrum...like, instead of what is your favorite spot/place at this high school, you could try, what is your least favorite spot/place at this high school? But don't generalize, ya know, don't make it too simple. I don't want you to say that this entire school is your least favorite place because that's too easy...that's too simple.

Class ends and I'm not able to explain why...like, why too simple is no good. I don't have time to verbalize my example because I hadn't thought of it yet...I didn't think of it until much much later.

For example, if I were to make this really broad statement about teaching, why it would be bad to do that because generalizing about teaching is like generalizing about students. Almost everything is right. Almost nothing is right. At its nucleus, perhaps, teaching is just another job, a paycheck, a means to a more immediate end, and yet any teacher will tell you, if they're really in it to teach and not just whore themselves out for another paycheck, that teaching in the most basic and purest of forms brings with a purposeful fulfillment to life. The good days far outweigh the bad. And when you have a really good day, there is always this immense feeling of accomplishment. The school is alive. The classrooms, the desks–everything. All around you things are not only living but learning, and you among them, and it is that progression of knowledge that makes you aware of this world that is so much larger than yourself.

Some days I feel this extreme, big picture awareness of this world I'm living in–where I am the most authentic form of myself, where I am, if only momentarily, the person I want to be. It's like, well...it's like in the midst of evil I want to be a good person. I want to treat others the way I would like to be treated without considering if they would do the same for me. I want justice and courtesy and respect, things I never knew I wanted when I was in high school. I want to be aware of these things all the time. Unfortunately, I'm not quite there yet.

So maybe I'm okay, but I'm not good enough...not yet.

Upon completing the necessary referral forms that afternoon, I realize I didn't even know the boys' names. Had to check with administration. Kind of funny though, after I'd gotten their names, and was writing my statement in carbon triplicate, the administrator handling the incident asked me a rather interesting question.

Administrator = Ryan, were they actually fighting? Both boys said they didn't hit one another. Insert a dumbfounded expression.
Briefly, I explain to her what had happened but she stops me before I even get to the bookcase part. She'd heard enough.

10 days OSS (out-of-school-suspension).

Left her office somewhat perplexed. Had I really stopped them from punching one another? Was that even possible considering everything that happened? A bit later, maybe even a good hour after school had been dismissed, I was the only one in my classroom when I heard the intercom go off above my head.

Intercom = Mr. Neumann...can you hear me?

Me = Uhhh...yep.

Intercom = Can you hear me clearly?

Internal Me = Crystal.

Me = Ummm...yeah, I can hear you.

Intercom = Ok, just checkin.

Me = Allllright.

Alright, great, you can hear me now.

XLERATOR

You can see Sponge Bob smoking a joint in green sharpie and smell...piss.

Stale piss in porcelain cups with excrement that runnith over. Toilet paper strewn across uneven tile footing. Ultra thin practical economics. Single-ply limitations.

The boys bathroom is adjacent to Room 300.

There is no door to the boys bathroom. Although, painted hinges suggest better days; days of four wall privacy. No paper towels; well, actually, there is toilet paper. Faucets spray treated water like a fire hose. The uh, hand dryer, otherwise known as the XLERATOR , is so loud the door to my classroom is consistently closed so as not to draw unneeded attention.

Gang signs written in multi-colored Sharpie decorate the white walls of the lavatory from time to time. But more often than not, such "expression" is quickly painted over with a fresh splotching of Behr brand flat white #11. Sometimes you can still smell the fumes.

The standard, "fuck this, fuck that, and...fuck you" spring up here and there. It just kind of depends on what stall you kick open; or rather, maybe I should say, it depends on which stall you open. Subtract the kick.

Anything and Everything can, will, and has gone down in the boys bathroom. I guess we can get into the specifics later on, but generally, you've got your fights, fight arrangements, drugs, gambling, hook-ups, graffiti, class skipping, "emergency" phone calls...and, well, more. This early in the semester the boys bathroom across from Room 300 is pretty quiet. Students, as well as teachers, are still sifting through all of the superficial congenialities. For the most part, the first two weeks of the semester, everyone is on their best behavior, or, at the very least, everyone is submissive enough for ritual compliance.

The late bell for 3rd block rang a little before noon. There was still someone in the boys bathroom. I knew this because of another unofficial duty I've acquired over the past year. Boys bathroom checker. Yes, it really is that glorious. Job description = check for sketchiness.

A 2-minute bell rings before every late bell; a subtle reminder to all that class will begin soon. 3rd Block is my planning period. With less than two minutes to go I enter the bathroom. All is clear except for one stall. The closest stall. Stall door is shut. I give it an inaudible push. Stall is locked. I don't say anything. Backup. Whoever is in there is standing, facing the industrial funnel. Colorful shoes. Heels facing towards me. The student is standing.

I walk out of the bathroom and prop myself up next to some lockers. The late bell rings. No one exits the bathroom.

2 more minutes go by.

"Does it really take that long to piss?" Maybe he's having a Tom Hanks moment; **A League of Their Own** and all that.

Cautiously, I walk back in. Stall door still appears to be shut and locked. Boy still standing. No sound. Nothing except for the cold air blowing through a window that has been forever painted open. Strange. I walk back out. What to do?

I decide to play the patient game and wait it out. He's got to come out sometime.

Another ten minutes go by.

"What the hell is this kid doing?"

Action thoughts begin to formulate.

Ok, what have I done before? Kick all the stall doors open from furthest to closest and scare him out of the stall? Punch a few knocks on the door? Press the white call button (never)? Create a blockade?

It seems a bit early in the semester to be turning the crazy switch on. Maybe I should just take the polite approach.

Polite it is. I walk back in. It's been about 15 minutes by now. Squat down like a catcher to make sure he's the only person in there. Still no noticeable noise coming from the stall so I say:

"Alright, whoever is in the stall, you have 1 minute to get out of there before we have problems."

"...w.hat?"

"You've got less than 1 minute to get out of that stall before you and I have problems."

I walk back out...again, and wait in the hall.

23 seconds later a boy appears. He's my height, probably weighs about the same as me and looks a little surprised.

Me = Soooo...(trying to find the words)...what, or, why have you been in there so long?

He seems kind of embarrassed. "..I..wassss...skipping lunch. I don't have money for lunch and didn't want to go in the cafeteria and not eat."

Me = Oh, well, dooo you need, or do you want to borrow some money for lunch?

"No it's OK. Not that hungry. I had a protein shake during weight training. I'll be OK til school gets out."

Me = Well alright, look man, oh hey, what's you're name?

"Tim. Timothy Johnston, sir."

"Nice to meet you, I'm Mr. Neumann." (insert handshake) "Look man, if you don't want to go to lunch that's fine by me, but you can't hang in the bathroom on the English hall. We've haddd...uh, problems up here lately. I'm not saying it's you or anything, but I don't want you to get in trouble. So, tell you what, we got this tiny computer lab that's pretty calm. It doesn't get much traffic during 3rd, so if you want to stay in there til lunch is over, I'll take you down there and write you a pass so you don't get hassled."

"Yes sir, that'd be good. Thanks. You said your name was Mr. Newman?"

"Yep, Newman. I teach right down there (insert pointing gesture) so if you ever need anything just stop by."

I swung by the little lab about 20 minutes later. Tim's lunch period was over by now and Tim should have been gone. He was, but he left a note:

Thanks Mr. Newman. -Tim

VERBAL VOMIT

I'ma get u like they did Biggie!

Jamal glares at me through a tiny portion of the window. It's the only part of the window that hasn't been smothered with scotch tape flyers. On days like this, I don't get much teaching done.

Weeessstttsssyyydddeee!!!

Jamal bobbles around spastically in the hallway as if he were unable to stand in one spot. I see this through the tiny window exposing fluorescent happenings in the hallway. He's mad because he's out in the hall again. Jamal has been in the hall 4 times (including this last one) today. Jamal has filter issues...that is, he chooses not to think, at all, before he speaks. He just kinda talks. It's like fucking diarrhea coming out the wrong end. Verbal vomit.

But let's go back to the future for a moment.

I never said if it was for a good or bad reason; the whole, "I need to speak with you thing." I just asked Jamal to step outside so we could talk. He froze instantly. Like, as soon as I asked him to get up his legs stopped working...and his mouth too. He was paralyzed. It was nice.

Me = Do you need some help?

Jamal looks up inquisitively and asks, "How u gonna help me get out my seat?"

There's so many different ways I could do this. Heart beats faster. Stay calm Neumann. Don't do it. Blood's circulating much faster now. Hands are red. Veins protruding across the back of both hands and then buried by clenched fists.

Me = Jamal....it was not a question.

Daniel chimes in from the back corner.

Daniel = Sound like a question to me.

The class laughs. It was kind of funny but I can't laugh because I am teacher...or something.

Daniel's wearing this black toboggan thing with rat fur lining the inside of each ear flap to keep his head extra warm. We're inside a 70 degree classroom with closed windows; not to mention 32 warm bodies. I'm thinking, "why the fuck are you wearing a hat?"

You'll have to excuse my language. Sometimes I leave school cussing just as much as my students.

I also don't enforce the hat dress code (no hats in school) very well.

Me = Jamal. Get up. Wait for me outside. I. will. not. ask. you. nicely. again.

Jamal slowly moves out of his seat and proceeds to walk out of the classroom. I don't see this happen though. I'm giving Daniel the stare down. We've been having a fantastically awesome day as well so naturally, he's staring me down too. He squints when he does this. Sizing me up. The rest of class sits as motionless middlemen in our awkward little standoff.

Daniel = Why u lookin at me like u wanna do sumpin?

Blood boils around the neckline. My head is about to explode from the inside out. Deep breath....

Me = Nothing man...nothing.....(deep breath) I need you to do a better job of (Daniel's eyes are wondering around the room at this point) listening when I'm talking.

Daniel = ...huhhh? wat?

Now back to Jamal.

He interrupts the stare down by punching the door to get my attention.

I'ma get u like they did Biggie! He points at me.

Me = Oh is that so.

I approach the door.

Jamal's staring at me and speaking into the door so I can't understand what he's saying. I'm pretty close to the door myself so I just lean over and stare right back at him. No blinking.

Slowly, I push open the door enough to hear what he has to say...but not enough for him to wiggle his way back into class.

His face becomes angelic right before saying, Lemme in Mr. Nueman...I need my jacket. CanIgemyjacket?...it's right ova der.

Me = Jacket?...(I glance around the room)...what jacket?

Ova der...my ROTC jacket.

Me = Ohhhh yeahhh, right. The jacket right over there (I point behind me and to the right). Ummm, yeah no I don't think so. Have fun in the hallway though (about to close the door when I pause)...oh and hey, don't you go runnin off on me ya here? (insert smirk) Alright man, be good.

3:21PM

The school day will be over in 4 minutes. Announcements that are rarely heard at a discernable decibel will cue everyone to pack up. The bell will ring. All will evacuate....but there's still 4 more minutes.

Can I do "this" for 4 more minutes?

Can I forget about all of "this" by tomorrow morning and start over? Happy? Idealistic? Patient? Willing to give it another go? Willing to roll with it...roll with the punches...with the lack of interest no matter how hard I try to make school better...the lack of respect?

WHAT HAD HAPPENED

The student's name was Audreanna. What had happened was, she arrived late to 1st block and handed me a note without saying so much as a word, and after about fifteen minutes I finally worked up the nerve to ask her what was wrong. Right away, her friend Dana spoke for her. I didn't understand pregnant teens. I was a new teacher then; I just didn't know. An argument, I thought, maybe even an upset stomach, so I listened to Dana when she looked up at me and said—She's not feeling well, just let her be for awhile—and then Dana put her arm around Audreanna and whispered something in her ear; inaudible melodies. Class proceeded with the normal disruptions, which are harmless unless you have a really strict teacher, and what I did was stand a few feet away from Audreanna who was under the watchful eye of her friend Dana. Whoever motioned for me to check on Audreanna midway through class must have been looking out for me. And if nobody had said anything, I very well could have been the first teacher in the history of public education to have a student deliver a baby in class.

It's all precisely accurate.

It happened, to me, nearly four years ago, and I still remember the girl's name and the "oh, shit" expression on my face and the soft humming sound of the air conditioner above our heads. I remember the smell of mold. Over in the English office there were three teachers on their planning period, but no resident nurses were in sight, and I remember the look of genuine intrigue spreading across the faces of my students as our attention fell undividedly to the pregnant girl.

Some students were flipping open their cell phones. Other students were dozing, or half dozing, and all around us were cement walls painted for that nondescript, eggshell white effect. Except for the giggly anticipation, things were quiet.

At one point, I remember, Dana turned and looked at me, not quite sure how to say it, as if to prepare me for the unexpected, and then finally she just spit it out, "Audreanna's been having contractions since she got here."

It's hard to say what exactly occurred next.

I was dumbfounded. There was a noise, I suppose, which must've been the white call button, so I glanced behind me and watched Audreanna raise her head from the desk and try to stand up. Her face was pale and reflective. She was so young. A junior in high school, short and compact, and when the EMT arrived it was so surreal, the way everything just seemed to stop as she was lifted onto a hospital gurney and rolled into the ambulance.

In any teacher story, but especially a real one, it can be difficult to distinguish what happened from what seemed to happen. What seems to happen becomes its own sort of, incident and ends up being told that way. The depths of perception are distorted. When the fire alarm goes off, your ears ring and you try to escape the decibels. When a girl goes into labor, you look away and then look back for a moment and then look away again. The images get shuffled; you miss a lot. I've heard psychologists refer to it as unintentional blindness. And then afterward, when you go to tell about it, there is always this fantastic authenticity about it, which makes the story seem fictional, but in actuality represents the very real and precise incident as it seemed. Majority of the time, a real teacher story cannot be believed. If you believe it, be skeptical. It's a question of credibility. In many cases the crazy shit is real and the commonplace blah isn't, because the commonplace blah is essential to make you believe the inconceivably crazy shit that occurs on a daily basis.

And then in other cases you can't even tell a real teacher story.

Sometimes, it's just beyond description.

For example, I tried telling my buddy this one a few years ago at Starbucks.

It was nearing the end of the school day and I was standing beside my classroom door along the narrow English Hall adjacent to the boys' bathroom. I remember how noisy it was. Class changes always are. Teenagers jostling back and forth, spilling over onto one another, moving without direction, and several young men crossed the hallway and marched into the boys' bathroom. The occasion seemed right for a fight.

"No joke," I said. "Six boys go into the bathroom and form a horseshoe around this kid who just got out of my class, his name was Alex. Real quiet kid too, just needed to use the bathroom before 4th block and he's washing his hands when this group of six pick him out of the cluster and box him in. The idea's to force Alex into fighting; just corner him so there's no way to escape. They're in a gang, but one of the kids wants out, so he has to ambush a complete stranger (Alex) or they're going to beat the shit out of him—doesn't matter who—they're just supposed to be there when it happens, whatever it takes, they say. Otherwise they're going to beat the shit out of the kid who wants out of the gang. Absolute ultimatum. No way out."

I glance at my buddy to make sure he had the scenario. I was playing with my plastic coffee top, pulling the lid off and on again, reading the caffeinated banter printed on the label.

My eyes were exhausted.

"We're talking gang-related directives. These six guys, they don't care who gets hurt. They don't have feelings. No emotions."

"That's pretty messed up," he says.

"I know," I said.

"So, then what?"

"Well, these guys get their black hoodies all zipped up, get the hoods up and over their heads to camouflage their faces a bit, and they wait for someone to throw the first punch and that's all they do, nothing else. One of 'em tries turning around other boys who are needing to use the bathroom but it's starting to get congested, some boys are forcing their way in and once they realize a fight is about to go down, they all want to stand in there for the 7 minute class change and watch. And man, I don't know–it's a little unsettling. This is school, right? But it's not like where we went to school. You don't know how unsettling some of this stuff is until you been there. Like the boy's bathroom...it's a bathroom, sort of, except there's really no privacy and the floor is always wet–like piss, except it's in places piss shouldn't be–everything's all wet and swirly and the toilet paper is all tangled up and thrown in the toilet so even if you did have to take a shit, you wouldn't want to because how are you going to clean up? And like, that day Alex wasn't even a person. He was just a mark...that kind of unsettling. But I guess I'm starting to realize you just go with that feeling–it's that sense of unease that takes you into these situations you wouldn't normally find yourself in...and the sound, man. The sounds carry forever. You hear stuff nobody should ever hear."

I was quiet for a second, just kind of tapping my empty coffee cup on the table, then I smirked a little.

"So after a couple minutes I start hearing this real muddled, kind of frenzied static. Weird echoes and stuff. Like a radio or something, but it's not a radio, it's this strange banter that's coming right out of the boys' bathroom. Faraway, sort of, but right up close, too. I was going over some make-up work with another student from Alex's class and tried to ignore the noise...because I should be focusing on this kid's needs. But it's right across the hall, right? So I listen. And with every step I take towards the bathroom, I keep hearing that crazyass noise. All kinds of onomatopoeia...ya know, like the old school Batman shit...BAM! POW! I mean, this is school–no way, it can't be real–but there it is, like every boy in that bathroom works for TMZ and is recording the fight on his phone. Before I see anything, I see hands in the air holding phones at just the right angle to capture the carnage. Then I see the blood. Naturally, I get nervous. One guy bolts by me with headphones in his ears. Another guy almost flips as he's trying to get by me and out of the bathroom. The thing is, though, I don't have anything to report yet. I can't just press the white call button and say, 'Hey, listen, I need some administrators up here, I think there might be a fight going on in the boys' bathroom.' I can't do that. It wouldn't go down. So I turn the corner around the entry way of the boys' bathroom and keep my mouth shut. And what makes it extra bad, see, is that poor Alex is totally outnumbered. Can't even get a punch in. Can't even yell for help because all the other boys are so much louder, he might as well have been whispering, and that aggravates the hell out of me. Not one person tried to help him."

Again there was some silence as I looked out the window. Evening was settling in, and out past the parking lot I could see cars driving in silhouette, through the strip malls and traffic lights.

"This next part," I said quietly, "you won't believe."

"Ha ha! Probably not," he said.

"You won't, man. And you know why?" I gave him a long, tired smile. "Because it happened. Because every word of this is an action, and because all of these actions create my words."

I made this sound in my throat, like a cough, but it was muffled, as if to insinuate that I didn't care if my friend believed me or not. But I did care. I still do. I wanted him to feel the realness, to believe the raw force of bystander indifference. I felt defeated, in a way.

"This kid, Alex," I said, "his face is pretty fucked up by the time I get over to them and try to break it up, and the only thing I can hear are voices behind me. Like football players in a huddle. That's what it sounds like, this big offensive line somewhere outside the bathroom. Cussing and chitchat and stuff. It's crazy, I know, but I hear the grunts. I hear the urgency in their voices. Real covert, all very organized, except this kind of thing isn't supposed to happen. This is school."

"Anyway, I try to be cool. Boys are scurrying out of the bathroom like roaches from Raid, but after a second I hear–you won't believe this–I hear rap music. I hear autotune and snapping fingers. I hear rhythmic whistling. Then after another second I hear sampled hooks and this weathered voice and all kinds of funky chanting and artificially automated shit. And the whole time, in the bathroom, there is still this fight going on. All these different voices. Not adult voices, though. Because this is school, ya know? The walls–they're watching. And the lockers, too, and the hallway security cameras and the damn cell phones. Everything watches and at the same time, it's like everything talks. The teachers talk politics, the students talk money. The whole school. Public Education. The institution talks. It talks. You know what I mean? So much of it–it's all-it's all gossip."

"Alex can't cope. He loses it. I don't know who to restrain. He gets up off the ground and begins shouting at the last boy who's frantically trying to make his way out of the bathroom–'what the fuck!' he says, 'why did you hit me?'–then he points at the kid who's shouldering his way past me. I get wide eyed and angry. There's no time to press the white call button. I can either stand there with Alex and wait for the administration to arrive so we can report the whole thing, or I can go after the kid who ambushed Alex and who's halfway down the staircase by now. And I'll tell you, it's in that moment that I just decided to say fuck it. Tell Alex I'll be back and I go after the kid, down the staircase. Against hallway traffic. He makes a break for it across the old gymnasium floor and through another set of double doors to a descending staircase. The warning bell rings. 2 minutes before 4th block starts. 120 seconds before I'm supposed to be teaching again. The kid's fast, for sure. But I don't know, must of been adrenaline or something cause I catch up to him like it's nothing. Like he's moving in slow motion or something. He reaches the descending staircase and is halfway down the first flight of stairs before I'm though the doors. Decide to take a leap of faith and jump for it. Reach out and grab for something in desperation. Somehow manage to get a strap on the kids backpack, plant my feet, and pull in the opposite direction; away from gravity. "What the fuck do you think you're doing!?!," I say. He's totally freaking out. Frantically trying to get away, about to slip off the backpack and make due without it, but I manage to get him into this stranglehold bear hug thing until he calms down.

"After a minute or two he finally gets quiet. Like you never even heard quiet before. One of those real heavy, yet real panicked moments, ya know, and here we are in this unmonitored stairwell–and everything's absolutely dead-flat silent. It's like we're there but we're not there–pure vapor, you know? All the established rules have been sucked into this unmonitored black hole. Not a single sound, except I can hear the kid's heart pounding.

"So I release him from the stranglehold and the kid starts talking. We walk up the staircase, back to the double-doors, and when we get there it's like verbal vomit. 'Please don't turn me in please don't turn me in pleasedon'tturnme in...they made me do it i had to do it or else or else i'm sorry ok i'm sorry i didn't mean it please don't turn me in...

I don't respond. Not a word. Like I've lost the ability to speak, but I'm thinking all these questions that I don't really want answers to like, what the hell happened up there? Why Alex? Why six against one? I'm exhausted, but I'm trying not to show it. I mean, I bust my ass trying to teach kids who've never even passed a high school English class before, and in between classes I'm supposed to deal with this shit? I want answers, I want to know what the hell happened. But the kid doesn't wanna give me specifics. So I just look at him for a while, sort of funny like, sort of amazed, and it feels like my whole understanding of what it means to be a teacher is right there in that stare. It says everything I've never been able to say. It says, kid, you got wax in your ears. It says, poor fuckin' kid, you'll never even know–wrong frequency–you don't even want to hear what I have to say. You're not even listening.

Finally, the kid gives me his name...Michael Kurby. Shake my head in disappointment. Meanwhile I've got twelve boys in my classroom, none of whom have earned any English credit whatsoever, so I shake the kids hand and walk away, because certain stories you don't ever tell.

You can tell a real teacher story by the way it never seems to end. Not now, not ever. Not after coffee that night. Not when I got into my car. Not even after I drove back into the city.

It all happened.

Even now, at this instant, I remember Alex's expression. In a way, I suppose, you had to be there, you had to hear it, but I can only imagine how desperately I wanted my buddy to believe me, my frustration at not quite getting the details right, not being able to stop the fight from ever happening, not quite pinning down the final and definitive reasons why.

I remember returning home alone that night, watching my own shadow disguise the locks to my front door, thinking about the coming day and how I would talk with Alex's father the next morning, all the things I might say to explain a situation I did not fully understand. Late that night I woke up in attack mode. Arms flailing. It just came to me...the moral, I mean. Nobody listens. Nobody hears anything. Like that kid who wanted out of the gang. The teachers, all the student types. My principal. Your principal. Everybody's critically important, yet easily replaceable, principal. What they need to do is go out and listen...ya know, instead of waiting for their turn to speak. Classrooms and corridors–you got to listen to all that.

And then again, in the morning, it all came rushing back to me. Couldn't escape. I was preparing to leave Castleberry Hill, checking my school bag, going through all the rituals that preceded the day's happenings. Already the sunlight was coming up over the abandoned railway building as a train was passing by, filing off toward the west.

"I got a confession to make," I said right before hopping into my car the night before. "That story, man, I had to make up a few things."

"Ha ha! I know that."

"The autotune. There wasn't any autotune."

"Right."

"No rhythmic whistling."

"Don't worry about it, Neumann, I understand."

"Yeah I know, but the rest, it's all real. Those six kids, they were like, wicked in there. And all the rest of 'em, just standing around, recording with their cell phones in there, you just plain wouldn't believe it."

"It's all right man, seriously, don't worry about it" he said, "but I mean, what's the point?"

For a long while I was quiet, looking away, and the silence kept stretching out until it was almost as if time stopped existing. Then I shrugged and glanced around the empty parking lot, into a space devoid of sound.

"The quiet– I guess. Just listen man, guess that's the point. There's always going to be plenty of noise in this world whether I say something, anything or not. Maybe in the end there is no point, but there's always quiet."

I threw on my backpack as the entrails of the previous night's conversation faded, closed my eyes for a moment, and let out a short, throat-clearing sigh. I knew what was coming.

That morning, closing the door behind me, I wondered if I could lock the quiet in.

THUGNIFICENT

National Education Committee

Friday Morning

Dear Friend,

Your immediate action is required.

Please carefully read and complete the enclosed **2010 Education Agenda Survey** which is **REGISTERED** in your name and affixed with a tracking code to ensure that it is accounted for in the tabulated results.

As Chairman of the National Education Committee (you don't need to know my name), I am sending out this questionnaire to gauge where you and other grassroots Educators stand on the critical issues facing our nation.

I need to hear back from you right away.

You know the noninterventionist elites as well as the unionized educator advocates are hoping you will put this letter down right now and do nothing...

...They want you to give up, desert your beliefs, and abandon the unique opinion that is your own. They want you to walk with them Ryan. They want you to drink the Kool-Aid.

Don't do it. **I'm asking you to please not turn your back on us** (it's OK, there is no us, this is actually a scam) **now**...

175 words comprise the statements stated above.

175 words +3 more pages of rambling bullshit =
No Postage Necessary

...Take just a few minutes to read and complete your REGISTERED copy of the **2010 Education Agenda Survey**, then make out your check or provide your credit card information in the space provided for your contribution of $500, $250, $100, $50 or even $30 (I'm a teacher dumbass...I have nothing to give you) to the National Education Committee, place it in the postage-paid envelope provided, and mail it right way.

The future of Education in this great country is in your hands.

Act now.

Sincerely,

Nicholas B. Hind (that's not my real name)

Chairman, National Education Committee

*DO NOT DESTROY * DO NOT DESTROY * DO NOT HATE*

"haters say what!"

"haters say what!"

"Stomp 'Em in The Nutz"

"Stomp 'Em in The Nutz"

Silence is somewhat of a rarity between the hours of 8:00AM and 4:00PM.

Me = John! What..in..the, what is that? What are we listening to?

I didn't even hear him walk in. What time is it?...3:45PM...damn I'm tired. What is that, 12 hours already? John's iPod is hooked up to the iHome over on my bookshelf. He's smiling from ear to ear, staring at me intently, waiting to see what my reaction is going to be.

John is laughing quietly. He turns up the volume so I can hear what I thought I heard only moments ago. Room 300 is on the very end of the English Hall which makes it possible for sound waves to roam with surprising clarity down the hall; especially when those halls are empty.

"HATERS SAY WHAT!"

"HATERS SAY WHAT!"

"STOMP 'EM IN THE NUTZ"

"STOP 'EM IN THE NUTZ!"

Me = Holy..crap...John! Turn that down! It's Friday man, teachers are bolting outta here just as fast as you guys. Seriously...what the heck man...not cool, totally not cool!

Slightly panicked, I get up out of my chair and start walking over to the stereo where John is standing. He turns the volume down so it's a little less than blaring and proceeds to break out in laughter.

John = AH HA HA hahahahaha!....Coach! Whew...coach! That's gotta be your theme song. Ha ha ha. Did you hear the chorus?...here wait a second, let me back it up for ya...

John quickly backs the song up about 10 seconds and hits play at a lower volume. He lip sings to the song and pretends like he's actually stomping some imaginary dude in the nuts.

I've known John for the past 4 years. He's matured a lot.

Logan walks in perplexed as to why John is laughing so much. Logan and John are both seniors and were the two most reliable runners I had on the Cross Country team this past year. They stop by Room 300 most afternoons to kill time, goof around, and play a few songs before Track practice.

Logan = Heey Coach. What's up with John? (John is on the floor laughing hysterically)

Me = Oh uh, he was just playing a song....who's it by John?"

John = Ha ha hah aha ha...huh?..oh, it's by Thugnificent.

Logan (instantly starts smiling) = Oh! What is it?...Stomp 'Em in The Nutz?

Welcome to Friday afternoon.

Logan= Play it again! Play it again John! Logan drops his backpack on the ground. John starts the song over again. Within seconds, there are 2 teenage boys lip singing and pretending to stomp imaginary haters in the nuts...in a variety of ways. I stand near the doorway; a mixture of laughter and "oh shit," I hope nobody walks by and sees this.

The custodian charged with cleaning the boys bathroom rolls up with her cleaning cart about 30 seconds later. She hears the song too. Instead of going about her work as normal, she pauses to see what's going on in my room. She sees me standing near the doorway. Behind me, she also sees two teenage boys jumping around the room pretending to stomp imaginary haters in the nuts.

Awkward.

Me = Song. Over. Now.

John and Logan quickly oblige my request. They see the custodian too.

Me = Look guys...(fighting back laughter)...I know it's Friday and all. But uh...maybe not the best song to play at a high volume, ya know?

They laugh and nod in agreement.

Me = I mean, this is exactly what I got an anonymous complaint about last year?...remember?

John = From who?

Me = ...um, a coworker...or, coworker(s)..I'm not really sure.

Logan = Ohhh....right. Sorry, Coach. You mean the time Jack was in here getting ready for practice and started blasting, "Because I Got High

Me = Exactly

John = Sorry Neums. Won't happen again.

Me = Ah ya know, whatever, it's cool...just try to be mindful of your musical selections.

John (laughing a little) = Did you like the song though?

Me = It was pretty hilarious. Who's it by again...Thug...?

John = Thugnificent and The Lethal Injection Crew.

Me = For real?

Logan = Yeah Coach, don't you ever watch Boonedocks?

Me = Nah man, can't say I've ever seen an episode. What channel is it on?

John = Adult Swim.

Logan = Yeah, I think it comes on Saturday nights at like, 12:00. You should totally check it out. It's like...like, uh South Park for Negroes.

Me = Logan!! Did you really just say that?

Logan = Yeah I know Coach. Politically incorrect (to say the least) I mean, I'm black though...I was just trying to give you a comparison...oh, before I forget (quickly changing the subject), here's a copy of that Owl City album I was telling you about (pulls CD out of his backpack).

Me = Oh sweet!..You remembered! Thanks man! I appreciate it.

Logan = No problem Coach. Hey John, we should probably get going. I need to call Shanice. Checkout this text she sent me.

John = Who's Shanice again?

Logan = You know, she's in Government with you. She's a little shorter than you. Pretty hot, but her teeth are kinda jacked.

John = Oh right! Shanice...on a scale of 1 to 10. What do you give her?

Logan = Ahuhh...7

John = 7!...really! That's pretty high for a girl at our school....we'll (checks his watch) We'll see ya Lund (that's me).

Logan = See ya Coach

Me = See ya guys.

Thugnificent.

GRAIN OF SALT

1 New Text Message.

Hi mr neumann. This is ali you just saw me yesterday with ana after school. I just wanted to tell you i just finished running six and a half miles at the gym. Because I remembered how you told us you ran five miles every day. Okay. Bye :) oh, and thank you for telling me that. It pushed me. The most Ive ever ran before today was two miles at one time.

SLEEPWALKER

(02:00AM)

Bite. Chew. Chew. Chew. Pause...what was that noise?
Eyeballs circle round the sockets. Cranium remains poised; securely
fastened to neck. Chew. Chew. Chew Chew chew
chewchewchew...swallow.

An empty plastic bag lays defeated and motionless on the kitchen
counter.

The time is 2:03AM.

Four chocolate chip cookies and one peanut butter and jelly sandwich
have gone missing by the time I become aware. That is to say, some
food has already gone missing by the time I realize where I am. The
stove light is on. Everything else in our place is dark. You can hear the
metal roll of a train gliding into the city. The windows are foggy. A
topless Tuperrware container resides next to the empty plastic bag on
the kitchen counter. Crumbs surround the area where the crime took
place.

Standing in the middle of the kitchen at...(check the stove clock)
2:04AM in my boxers.

Damn it, sleepwalking again. Well hold on a sec (glance down at the counter), make that sleepeating too.

Great, that was my lunch. At least I won't be hungry later.

(PAUSE)

I've been sleepwalking and uhhh, (mumble) sleepeating for as long as I've been teaching. I never really know when it's gonna happen. I never really know what I'm going to eat either. Sometimes it's a loaf of bread (yes, that's right, an entire loaf)...sometimes it's cookies (whole box), a bag of chips (we're talking the family size here), and then there's crackers, leftovers...but then sometimes it's just a coke or the healthy choice; water.

Four years of sleepwalking with various levels of coherence. I've gone months at a time without finding myself perplexed as to why I am sitting upright on the couch at 4 in the morning, and then I've done the whole zombie thing every day for an entire school week. Mara's told me I talk too. Whenever she tells me about my social inclination the next morning I'm like, "oh shit, what did I say?" Apparently I lie a lot when I'm incoherent. I'll wake up randomly at, I don't know, 3:37 in the AM and Mara will hear me get up. She'll ask, "what are you doing Neums?" Instantly I reply with, "going to get some water." Guess that's my default answer. But Mara knows me better than that. She'll think or say, "bullshit," because she knows I'm not going to get water. For some reason, my deranged sleepwalking self doesn't want to tell her I'm going to binge eat and then come back to bed. So, instead I lie and recite the water line while walking to the kitchen so I can proceed with gluttonous consumption.

STICK 'EM UP!

I love Paris in the the spring.

1:55PM to 3:25PM = 4th block (last class of the day)

I love Paris in the the spring.

10 minutes into class I realize I don't have enough copies for today's activity.

Me = Mr. Pluck, I just realized I don't have enough handouts for our next activity. Would you mind if I stepped out for a moment to make some copies? (It's not really a question. I'm going to walk out that door one way or the other and Mr. Pluck is going to keep an eye on 'our' class. I just phrase it as a question to be polite.)

Mr. Pluck and I teach one class together. This is commonly known as Co-Teaching. Long story short, Mr. Pluck and I are both supposed to teach 9th grade literature to 33 students.

Mr. Pluck = Dhh...what was that?...oh yeah yea, copies. Sure, sure...go head. I think I can keep my eye on...(shifting his attention to the 9th graders seated behind me) HEY!...ARIEL!...R...E....L.....I TOLD YOU (an aside to me) why can't they keep their hands to themselves…I TOLD YOU, NO LOOK, I TOLD YOU TO STOP MESSING AROUND! KEEP YOUR HANDS TO YOURSELF!

Internal thoughts = Are you f…Don't cuss. Deep breath. My god, look the other way Ryan. Look down. Stop listening. Doesn't he see it?… They're 9th graders and it's the last class of the day. Can't expect them to sit in their fu…(don't cuss) seats all day.

Mr. Pluck = Now where were we?…

After a verbal thrashing the boy and girl sitting next to each other continue to joke around. We're talking grade school flirtation here. Stealing each other's pen. Crumpling up one another's handout. Giggling and all that hormonal awkwardness.

Mr. Pluck =…You want me to make the copies while you get started with the writing?

Internal thoughts = Holllyyy shi (don't cuss)…listen man! Pay attention!

Me = Umm no, not quite. I'll make the copies real quick…and you can tell the students how we're dividing class into 2 different groups just like last week.

Mr. Pluck = Right…

He points both index fingers at me. Like he's giving me the 'thumbs up' only with his pointer fingers.

Mr. Pluck = So, let me see if I got this right…

Class is completely off task. No learning. No teaching. I'm repeating directions for the third time to my co-teacher. Potential energy is slowly transforming a room full of 33 ninth graders into kinetic disarray.

Mr. Pluck = …I'm going to stay in here with my reading group from last week. We'll uh, we'll finish the worksheets from the consumables (consumables = workbooks) and then what?

Me = (Don't let him see the mounting irritation) Class will be over.

Mr. Pluck = No it won't. This (points to the worksheets) will only take about 15 minutes.

Me = Well then you can do this. I point to the writing activity I'm trying to make copies of.

It all seems so clear in my mind. Turn burner to HI heat. Heat blood until mounting pressure brings blood to a boil. Continue boiling blood until top button of shirt shoots like bullet from gun. Button will decimate anything in its path.

Mr. Pluck stands directly in front of me...rambling in an audible stream of consciousness.

Me = That's true. Ok, so how bout this...You will take half the class down to the open computer lab. Today, you will take my group from last week (I point to one half of the class). Soooo...I had the writing group stay up here, with me, in this room last week. They are done with the writing activity. They all finished it last week. So, you can take my writing group from last week downstairs and walk them through the short story that was also assigned last week. They have not read this story yet, but you have. You did this activity last week with your group. So, since you already know the story, know the reading activity, the only thing that will be different for you, today, are the students. Make sense?

Mr. Pluck = No, but OK, let's go with it.

Somebody please stab me with a spoon.

Me = You sure? (He nods yes) Ok, well let me go run these copies for the writing activity real quick. Can you hold down the fort for like...3 minutes?

Mr. Pluck = Sure Ryan.

He gives me a little pat on the shoulder, like, "no problem kid."

Exit stage right.

Copier on the English hall is broken...again. Office Space allusion. "Paper jam! How come it says paper jam when there is no paper jam? I swear...." OR "...PC Load letter...what the f...(don't cuss)

Walk downstairs to the mailroom. No one is using the copier...thank goodness. The feeder tray that delivers copies into the actual finishing tray is busted which means your options are to rig up some crazy MacGyver contraption or kneel down to catch the copies in your hand.

There's always time for MacGyver. Copies made. Frantically power walk back to class so as not to lose anymore instructional time. I open the door...pause in disbelief...actually step back out with copies in hand to check the room number and make sure I'm in the right classroom...yep, right number, and then take 1.5 steps back inside.

Mr. Pluck = Now raise your hand...come on now, when I tell ya'll to stick 'em up, that means you gotta raise your hands high so I can see 'em. Who thinks this old man up here (referring to himself) can't stand on his hand for 10 seconds? Stick 'em up!

Most hands raise. Some students sitting in the back kind of inch up out of their seats to see if this is really about to happen...if this self-proclaimed old man is really going to stand on his hand.

Mr. Pluck = Well alright, now don't forget when you go home tonight to tell your folks what you learned at school today.

33 ninth graders sit in quiet anticipation. Waiting for a spectacle. Wishing for broken bones. Hoping for a good story to tell their friends. It's written all over their faces. I'm standing in the doorway with 35 copies of a writing activity that will go unused.

Mr. Pluck bends down. Knees bend in a gradual motion to allow greater reach. He lifts up his right shoe ever so slightly, places the majority of his right hand underneath the bottom of his shoe, and lowers the shoe.

1...2...3....4...5....6....7.....

students ease back into their seats...8....9.....disjointed chatter grows louder by the second.....10.

Internal thoughts = What the f...! Have I just entered a fucking carnival! You've gotta be shitting me!

Mr. Pluck = Oh Mr. Neumann. Welcome back, I was just giving them a demonstration on...(bla bla bla I can't hear the next part because I'm wondering if my eyes are actually going to pop out of their sockets)....oh but, I thought this might be a great discussion starter. Here, I was passing this sheet of paper around the room and having the students read it out loud...what does this say? (He points at the paper)

I've forgotten what subject I teach.

The tattered piece of scratch paper reads, "I love Paris in the the spring."

I say (reading as fast as I possibly can),

"IloveParisinthespring."

Mr. Pluck = "What was that? What'd you say?"

Me (louder and slower) = I love Paris in the spring.

Mr. Pluck = Ya hear that class. Mr Neumann read, I love Paris in...the spring.

Some kids laugh a little. They already know. They've completed this exercise where as I, have not.

Mr. Pluck grins and chuckles a bit. He turns so that we're side by side, facing the same direction. He then reads the line scrawled on the tattered paper one more time, pointing with his index finger as if to underline each word..."I...love...Paris...in...the....the....spring."

Mr. Pluck = Ya see, there's 2 of 'em (pointing to the).

Me= Ohhhh wow. You're right....I didn't catch that (insert sarcastic undertones).

Mr. Pluck = Well nobody does. See that's the point. Ya know if we had a smaller class or even, a quieter bunch, I might be able to have an actual discussion about stuff like this instead of using it as a parlor trick to keep the class in order.

Me= Yeaaaa...(don't say it Ryan. Nod and smile. Nod and smile. Don't worry...you'll figure out it out. You'll find a way to make this class work)...good point.

I slowly step away and walk over to other side of the classroom.

Internal thoughts = Slow, controlled breathing, come on man, you can do this. Time to introduce the lesson.

I roll up 35 handouts to form one solid cylinder. Look down and close my eyes for a second. Pretend the papyrus pipe is a shotgun and blow my brains all over the dry erase board.

I love Paris in the the spring.

I love pretending I'm a a teacher.

I love pretending I'm a teacher.

I'm a teacher.

I am a teacher.

GONE FISHIN

"A man tells so many stories, that he becomes the stories. They live on after him, and in that way he becomes immortal."

Roll credits. Lights On.

Big Fish (Tim Burton, 2003, check it out!) = Over.

32 eleventh graders. 20 minutes until class ends. What to do now...?

They all assume class is over. Students begin to meander from one table to the next...migrate from one corner of the room to the other...sit on top of desks or abandon sitting altogether.

A few students are frantically trying to complete a previous writing assignment so I scoop those up when they're ready, lay the papers on my makeshift table desk, and stand in front of my class, waiting for their undivided attention.

I have absolutely no idea what I'm going to say.

Clouds move in an animated watercolor leftrightleftright outside Room 300. It's been raining quite a bit this morning. Nobody really notices me standing there. I continue to stand...waiting...and waiting; I've never been much of a yeller.

Still don't know what to say but know I need to find the words fast.

A few more seconds pass and I just decide to let the words run like a faucet.

Me = Alright folks...we still gotta few minutes left so don't go packing up quite yet. Please find your seats and sit back down...I've got a couple more questions to ask you.

I really don't.

Some students groan...others roll theirs eyes...and the more active participants take their time in regaining their sedentary position.

Me = Ok, so....well, first off, what'd you guys think of the movie?

Class = It was good!...good...no response...is class over yet?....it was awight...good, yea I like it.....it sucked...just kiddin...it was pretty good...and so on and so forth.

Begin nonsense.

Me = Alright cool cool...ya know, I like it a lot and there are a lot of similarities between this movie (I point at a now blank projector screen) and the Native American origin myths we read last week (nice! go me)...but as far as the movie goes, there's one line that I reaaallllyyy like and I tried to write it down but, of course, go distracted so I don't know if this is exactly how it goes but....the closing line in Big Fish = A man tells so many stories, that he becomes the stories. They live on after him, and in that way he becomes immortal...

Class = Listening and wondering why I'm wasting their time with this ramble.

Me = ...ya know, it's a neat way to look at life and the whole idea of immortality. If we conclude this statement to be true (uh oh, I might be on to something) man can truly be immortal...even though, one day...we're all gonnaaa...come to the end of the line...

Really, I'm stalling. I have absolutely no idea what I'm going to do for the next 15 minutes. I am ramble.

Glance outside...it's still raining but not as hard. Look back at the class and then it clicks... he becomes his stories.

Hot damn that's it!

Me = ...so that last line of the movie reminds of something that happened last year. Actually, it was almost a year ago to this day (not really), I was planning on being out on a Friday. So, ya know, I put in for a sub, and you all know what the means...you get some random worthlessness who sits in the front of the room and texts all day...a great role model to say the least.

A few laughs.

Me = So, generally, teachers are supposed to leave sub plans...but on this particular occasion I just decided to say screw it, and I didn't leave anything. I didn't tell any of my classes I was going to be absent and just left a stack of papers for them the next day. It was supposed to be like, a stack of letters, or a memo or something.

Class = intrigued

Me = In the letter, and you may have heard about this...it said that I was indefinitely suspended from teaching because of my unorthodox teaching methods.

Class = some kids blurt out, Oh yeah! I heard about that. Others nod in agreement.

Me =Ok cool, so some people know and for those who don't, the letter said I was suspended indefinitely and the only way to get me back, if indeed anyone wanted me back, by Monday, was to write a persuasive letter to the County Board of Education by the end of the day, that Friday...after that, it was supposed to be kind of like a waiting game.

Class = listening...like, really listening.

I continue telling the story but walk to the window in the back of the room, unlock it, and open it. I then proceed to walk back to the front of the room, to the other window, unlock it, and open it. A cool breeze flows in and you can hear the rain falling.

Me = So here's the thing...the whole letter my students found and read about me being suspended and this and that...it was fake...I wrote it myself.

Class = silent

I use the moment of quiet awkwardness to walk back to the back of the room and grab this long metal pipe (don't ask why) that I have stored behind a whole bunch of teaching books I don't use.

Walk back to the front of the room.

Me = Now look, you guys are the first to know it was all made up, so you can tell whoever you want, but I need you to think about this, how does this change your idea of truth? I tap the pipe on the tile floor.

Me = So like, if you were one of my former students, one of the students who thought I was really suspended they would probably tell you it's true...that yes, I was suspended, because he or she had an actual letter in front of them saying that very thing.

Pick up the pipe and hold in both hands.

Me = But now, here you are...you know something they never knew. You now know it was a lie and that I wrote the suspension letter myself....so, something I really need you to think about...how does this change your thoughts on the whole idea of truth?

Me = Is truth fact?....or is it subjective.

Class = What does subjective mean?

Me = Uhhh...well, it kind of means it can change, like my version of truth is going to be different than your version of truth but that's ok...it just kind of varies depending on the person.

Internal thoughts = Is that right?...well, whatever.

Me = Oh hey, before I forget, do we got anyone who's good at tying knots?

Class = silent and reluctant.

Ask for participation and sometimes you get paralysis instead.

A male student sitting near the front cautiously raises his hand.

Me = Awesome! Alright...here ya go (I hand him the metal pipe), I'm gonna go fishing but I need some fishing line....so (I unfasten the top button of my shirt, loosen the tie, remove the tie, and hand it to the student)...sir, I need you to securely fasten this to the pipe.

Class internal thoughts = what the hell is this whackjob doing?

The student fastens my tie to the pipe while I scribble something on a sheet of paper.

Me =Now if I'm going fishing, I gots to have bait...so here, written very badly on this sheet of paper, is my bait....

I turn the sheet of paper around so the class can at least see I've written something and read my bait aloud.

Student = It's upside down Mr. Neumann.

Me = That's cool man, fish can read upside down...didn't you know that?

Sheet of paper = "What is Truth?"

Me = Alright, so, even if you can't read the sign, you know what I'm fishing for...truth.

At this point, the pipe tie fishing rod is ready to go so I thank the student and he hands me the fishing rod.

Class = WTF

I grab some masking tape and wind it around the sign and tie so as to do the whole adhesive thing.

Me = Now here's what I'm gonna do...I'm goin fishin.

I hold on to the pipe and cast the tie out the window with my bait attached...secure the pipe to a nearby filing drawer and say the following:

Me = ...now, that fishing pole is going to stay outside all day and all night...until I catch something. Tomorrow, when you guys come back to class, there's going to be something on the end of my line, or....tie. I will have caught some sort of truth but you need to make sure you think about the question too!...What is truth?

Class = laughing in disbelief.

Me = Oh hey, well hold up, how much time do we have left?...2 minutes...damn!...or darn, whoops, OK, just enough time for one last thing.

I walk over to the back window and ask the students sitting near the window to step aside. I step up on a chair and put one foot on the open window.

Class internal thoughts = Is he going to jump out the window?

Me = Something you guys also need to keep in mind...there's isn't a right or wrong answer to this question. Everyone's answer will be different. Now wait here for a sec, and whatever you do, do not follow me.

I disappear out the window.

Maybe I should have said this earlier, but my classroom is above ground level.

Class internal thoughts = where did our teacher just go?

Thud. From inside the classroom, everyone hears a wet thud.

Class internal thoughts = our teacher just jumped off the roof. Our teacher is suicidal. Our teacher might be dead.

A few moments later, I appear at the other window where my fishing line is. I hold the bait, What is Truth?, and project inward to the classroom.

Me = Everyone has their own version of truth. What you guys need to remember, what you guys need to realize, is that truth means different things to different people. We will all have a different answer to this question and there's no telling what kind of answer I'm going to have waiting on the end of this tie tomorrow morning....

Internal thoughts = What the hell am I going to have on this tie tomorrow morning?

GET DAT MONEE

A black wallet lies unattended on the newly renovated flooring of Room 300.

It's my wallet...wasn't quite sure how to start off class today. Didn't really feel like talking though...and, well I guess this is just my opinion, but, talking...like, teacher talking, is a highly overrated instructional commodity when it comes to relating information to high school students in a retainable way.

32 students are sitting in my educational apartment anticipating some sort of transition. We've finished the standard introductory lesson for the day...well, not me, but my very capable co-teacher...

(I'm being serious about this one...I have two co-teachers this semester and the one I'm mentioning now, well...we've been working together on and off for the past 3 years and kind of have a system down. I say kind of because there really isn't a set system...I change my mind way too much for that kind of structure)

...but yeah, anyways,

students + transition + me standing in front of classroom:

I walk over to the computer bag residing in the chair I don't sit in, unzip the front pouch, and grab my wallet. I walk back to my public speaking spot and extend my right arm so that it looks like I've just completed a full Nazi salute.

Wallet (black) in my right hand. Glance at my wallet, then at the ground, then back at my wallet. Brain tells hand to release grip and wallet falls to ground.

A few students take notice but for the most part, everyone else is politely carrying on separate conversations.

My black wallet lies stranded on the newly renovated flooring of Room 300. I turn my back to both the wallet and my class, take a few steps towards the projector screen, yank on the handle so as to pull the screen up and reveal the dry erase board.

There are 3 statements scrawled in fading blue EXPO:

1. I am 27 years old.

2. I have zero functioning credit cards.

3. When I drive to work each morning, I think about skipping my exit, skipping work, and driving West. For about 30 seconds each morning, I pretend my wife is with me and we've decided to leave everything and just...drive.

I turn around and the students are beginning to pay attention.

My wallet is still on the floor.

Me = I.....am.....27....years...old.

I don't ask for everyone to be quiet...or stand until there is an overwhelming silence...I just read directly from the board.

Me = I am 27 years old. (insert shrug) Who thinks, well wait, this (point at board)...is a sentence right? Like, it's declarative...it's stating that I am 27 years old, right?

Class = Head nods. A few people look at me, look at the board, then back at me. They're trying to figure out if I look 27.

A student in the back kind of cocks his head to the side, squints, and says, "Mr. Neumann, I don't know, are you...28?"

Others start chiming in.

"Nah...he's not that old. What are you like, 22 or 23 Mr. Neumann?"

Other students = I think he's 27. You look 27 Mr. Neumann...yeah.

Me = Who thinks the first statement I have written up here on the board is true?

Class = I do....yeah me too...I do...yeah...head nod...totally passed out on desk...yea...why wouldn't it be true?...

Me = Well...how do you know. Where's your proof? What...are you just gonna take my word for it?...you're just gonna believe me...I tell you I'm 27 and you take that to be true?

Class = Well yeah...some don't know what to say but seem intrigued at least...why would you lie to us?...you're the teacher...yeah, why would you lie?

Me = Well, I mean, first of all...you guys already know I've lied before (read Gone Fishin if you don't know what I'm talking about). But I don't know...maybe I think lying is funny...maybe I want to see how many of you are just going to blindly believe everything I say...(insert shrug)...but seriously, you don't know. How would you know if I'm actually 27? You have no proof.

Class = Contemplating...what the hell is the point of all this?...it's Friday man, don't make us think...hmmmm...

I pick my wallet off the floor, open it up, and extract my driver's license.

Me = Ok, check this out. Here's my driver's license (insert Vanna White swivel)...now if we take that first statement, I am 27 years old and you had my driver's license in your hand, you could verify that right?...you could look at my birth date and figure out if I was 27?

Class = Head nods...yea....yeah....sleeper (middle of class)...

Me = Alright, cool.

I drop my wallet back on the ground and throw my driver's license across the open floor space like a stone across water.

Class = Full attention....except for the sleeper.

Me = Yesterday, I went fishin, right? So, if you weren't here yesterday, I basically made a fishing pole out of my tie and a metal pole.

Absentees = What?...what were you fishing for?

Me = Well, I had a question and I went fishing for an answer?

Absentee = Are you serious?

Me = (nod my head from left to right as if to indicate 'No')...totally. So anyway, over here, just like yesterday, is my fishing pole hanging out the window. Now I know some people saw me yesterday afternoon and you may have been wondering why the fishing pole wasn't out the window....

Majority of class internal thoughts = I don't know what you're talking about Mr. Neumann.

Me = Well, yesterday I caught something...and in the process (this better be good Ryan)...the line broke. So, I had to bring the fishing pole in. When I got here this morning I threw a longer line out the window to see if I could catch anything else and I did! So, turns out I've got two things to show you.

Walk over to the window, raise it up a bit more so it's easier to lift my answers in the classroom. Reel up the tie to reveal a plastic grocery bag. I loosen the knot on the brown Kroger bag to separate it from the tie and walk back over to my preaching spot. As I'm walking over I notice two things:

1. I can actually hear the plastic crunching noise that accompanies bag movement which means...class is quiet...I look around and notice that everyone (minus the sleeper of course) is listening.

2. There also appears to be a new body in Room 300. An administrator...oh shit...heart race picks up a bit...shit...there is no C.Y.A. (cover your ass) paperwork splattered anywhere...no lesson objectives...no essential learning questions...no performance standards...just white walls, me with a plastic grocery bag, 32 quiet students, 1 co-teacher...and 1 administrator...oh shit oh shit!
I pull a dictionary out of the recycled plastic whatever.

Me = Ok...so, the first thing I caught...a dictionary....and!...this will be important for later...headphones. It appears these headphones are marking two different pages.

I open the dictionary to a phonemarked page.

Me = So...it looks like we have a definition for the word 'truth' here...

I must have pulled the projector screen back down...definitely don't remember doing that but I quickly type up some basic notes about the truth definition and project them onto the screen; asking the students to jot these notes down because they'll need them later.

As they're still scribbling down the notes I highlight one of six short definitions found in the dictionary...something about fact, reality, and statements that are believed to be factual and/or true...thank you Webster.

I pull the projector screen back up to reveal the second statement.

Class =...Hey!...I wasn't done copying yet...what the......

Me = No worries...you can get the definitions later...I need you to look at this second statement...I have zero functioning credit cards.

Me = Based on what you've been learning about me, today...how many people would believe this second statement to be true...raise your hand.

Class = A few hands raise...others are hesitant...some verbally say NO or nod their heads...then there's the sleeper...she's sleeping.

I walk back over to the window and pull my second answer through the window. Tie connected to belt, belt connected to extension chord, extension chord attached to a sheet of paper with writing on it.

I rip the piece of paper off the plug, show the words to the class first, and then read my second answer aloud...Truth is not a definition.

Class = ...WTF...this guy is way too f-ing weird....

Let go of the answer, it floats to the ground and I decide to pick my wallet back up and do the Vanna White thing one more time...this time showcasing the internals of my wallet.

Student = Hey I see a credit card...yea me too...you're lying again.

Me = Oh you mean this...nah you're close, this is my debit card....not quite a credit card.

I take my debit card out and chuck it across the floor much like I did my driver's license...which I notice is being passed around the room from student to student.

The debit card is quickly confiscated by another student. A couple boys are looking it over when my co-teacher kindly walks over and asks for the card before they get any crazy ideas (thank you Mr. J). It then occurs to me that this might be a good time to clean out my wallet.

Me = So...what else do I have in here?

All sorts of cards start flying out of my wallet; skipping stone ammunition. Business cards, membership cards, Chicago train stub, D.C. train stub, MARTA card, home insurance information, heath insurance group number...all scattered there in front of me; gravity fastening rectangular possessions of my life to the dirty floor.

I give a brief description of each item, heaving some blindly towards the trashcan (movie gallery, blockbuster)...students are starting to laugh now. Before you know it, my wallet appears to be empty.

Me =....Oh!...I forgot to tell you. I don't have any cash either...check it out (open wallet. behold emptiness)...got one receipt from dinner last weekend.

Student = So you really don't have any credit cards?

Me = Not exactly. Here....lemme get this out of this little (I'm trying to get something out of one of those little inside wallet pockets that you use for like, your house key...or maybe business cards from contacts you will never contact) pocket.

Students laugh as I struggle to remove the items. Damn plastic pieces got stuck in the corner of the pocket...finally, the struggle pays off.

Me = (holding 4 pieces of plastic in my left hand) I used to have an American Express card and a Mastercard...but...it got to the point where I was using these cards for anything and everything. So...about 2 months ago I decided enough was enough. I grabbed a scissors and cut my credit cards in half. Then I told myself that I was not, and will not, use these credit cards again until I've paid off all of my debt.

I transfer the 4 pieces of plastic, 1 at a time, from my left to right hand and then pour them onto the floor as well.

Me = So, the second statement (point behind me and to the screen) about having zero functioning credit cards is...true.

Student = You're an organ donor Mr. Neumann

Me = Am I?

Students = That's what it says on your license.

Me = Oh!...huh...well, guess I am then. Cool. Now onward to the last statement.

When I drive to work each morning, I think about skipping my exit, skipping work, and driving West. For about 30 seconds each morning, I pretend my wife is with me and we've decided to leave everything and just...drive.

Me = This last statement is up to you. You can choose to believe me or not believe me. Statements like this are tricky because unless you know the person, know kind of...how they act and what their sense of humor is all about...it could be hard for you to determine the ummm, realness of the statement.

Me = Mood and Tone are super important when considering a statement like the last one I've written up here. I can say it again a different way for added reinforcement, like, "No joke...there are days, like this morning...I was driving to work and thinking I could just say, F-it, and keep on driving."

The class laughs...hearing teachers almost cuss = comedy.

Me = But you still don't really know if I'm telling you the truth. Now I've got like one more thing for you to...uh, listen to, and then we'll get on with the assignment...this last thing relates to the headphones I used as a bookmark.

I pull out my iPod, turn it on, pick out a previously selected song and insert the black 80G into the iHome behind me and to the left.

Me = We've got this third statement...about me not coming to work...and I think it's kind of hard to determine the sincerity of it because we don't know the 'real' mood OR tone.

Finger on the Play button.

Me = Now I'm gonna play the first 30 seconds of this song by the Dave Matthews Band called, You and Me...the only thing I need you to do is listen...try to really hear the words because that will be the tone...but don't forget about the music either because that's the mood.

Class = ...Who is this...Dave what?...

Me = Look, here's the idea. I am trying to use a song to communicate the same idea I've written here in this third sentence on the board...So, it's like I'm using music that I like, to express a small truth about myself without writing or saying anything of my own.

Play. Pause. Stop. Talk of tone. Talk of mood. Talk of truth. Due date assigned...2.3.10...Erik's birthday (not an accident). Project assigned.

Administrator leaves with a smile.

Students begin phase 1 of project with remaining class time. I grab my fishing pole and head back over to the window...secure it to the filing drawer, and proceed to pitch the tie, belt, and extension chord back out the window.

Student = Goin fishin again Mr. Neumann?

Me = Yep.

Student = Watcha tryin to catch?

Another student = ...by the looks of his wallet, I'd say he needs to go fishin for some money.

Students nearby laugh.

I laugh.

Me = Nah man, money sucks...not the biggest fan of money...

Precious = I am Mr. Neumann... it's my birthday and the only reason I'm here today is to get dat monee!

Precious is bubbly. She laughs and I say happy birthday.

Student = Well if you don't want money, which is just weird!...what are you trying to catch.

Me =I don't know man...(pause to contemplate) yea, I don't know...maybe ideas for next week.

Student = you don't know what we're doing next week?

Me = I didn't even know what we were gonna do today...

Student = For real?...

Me = Maybe

Ryan Lund Neumann

COMATOSE

To: FACULTY

From: PRINCIPAL

Subject: PERSONAL LIFE VS. PROFESSIONAL LIFE

In an era overrun with technological advancement and innovation, the rules pertaining to social communication have forever changed. As a result, the implications of social networking and more specifically, social networking sites, continually challenges the boundaries of both our personal and professional lives.

As administrators, we find ourselves investigating correspondence delivered via the internet OR transcribed on social networking sites on a more and more regular basis.

Hello Big Brother.

The intention of this email is not to warn you of wrong doing, but rather, to alert you of issues affecting your colleagues within AND outside of our district.

Numerous teachers utilize Myspace, Facebook, Twitter, blogs, and Youtube. As teachers and educators, it is critically important that you understand the repercussions these technological forums can have on your careers.

* **As a general rule, DO NOT post, write, or print anything you DO NOT want to come back and haunt you one day.**

* Why do I suddenly feel nervous?

* **Remember, with social networking and the internet ...nothing is ever totally private. However, at the very least, be sure to employ private features...not public.**

* **Separate personal life from professional life**.

* ......Ryan, you know the drill...no profanity......

* **DO NOT mix personal life and professional life.**

* **Mixing the two, especially on social networking sites, can have dire consequences.**

* **Please know who has access to your sites.**

For further inquiry, direct all questions and concerns to School Board policy IDK-OMG-WTF.

4:00AM

Slap phone off bed...not the alarm...damn...blindly grope nightstand area where alarm resides...turn off alarm. Fumble around for glasses. Pick up phone. Press button on phone in an attempt to illuminate screen and verify the AM nature of this coherent visit.

Key Lock

Now press *

*

Keys Unlocked

49 New Text Messages

Readjust spectacles.

49 New Text Messages...

I wrote my phone number on the dry erase board during class yesterday. Guess you could say I like giving my students options.

Option 1 = Read story, answer questions on separate sheet of note book paper, complete by the end of class, have a nice day.

Option 2 = Read story, paraphrase portion of story, create a text message of your paraphrase, be sure to include your name, and text your message to me (Neumann) by 11:59PM.

4:00AM

49 New Text Messages

Please know who has access to you.

I don't even know who has access to my phone number but ya know what, that's fine by me.

9:31PM

Wake up on chase lounge at home. Damn it!...I was only going to nap for an hour.

Some nights, after eating dinner, that's it for me; like....game over, lights out, check ya later. Food Coma.

What is a Food Coma?...you may ask yourself.

Food Coma = School day proves to be rather exhausting for one reason or another...eat dinner with Mara (one of my favorite parts to any weekday)...worry about sleepwalking/sleepeating....end up eating more in an attempt to subside my pathological lying sleepwalker self

from rising like a vampire in some cheesy ass low budget gothic
flick...and pass out on the couch within 10 minutes of eating dinner.

Typically, this happens towards the end of the week but seeing as how
it's only Tuesday, I'm not entirely sure what's going on.

9:31 PM

Wake up on chase lounge and logic doesn't register. It feels like
someone took a vacuum cleaner to my eyes and sucked out all the
moisture. Contacts feel like shards of plastic from the six-pack soda
rings you typically don't cut up before throwing away because
normally you don't care if the fish get caught in the rings and die but
for some reason you cut the plastic up today and now two pieces, one
for each eye, have somehow managed to replace your contacts and
impair your vision.

It feels like double stick tape; only one side of the tape is stuck to my
cornea.

Mara = You're phone was just ringing.

Me = (still sleepy/waking up...not entirely aware of anything)...huh?

Mara = You're. phone. was. just. ringing.

Me = Oh!..that's weird. Thanks.

Mara = No prob babe.

1 missed call.

1 New Voice Message

Neeuummmaannnnnn....Neeuuummaaannnn!!...Now, Neumann...I
hope you're a man of your word and call me right back...just like your
voice message box promises...call me back Neumann....I know you told
us not to call after a certain hour but since I'm not your student
anymore, I decided that rule didn't apply to me...

Separate your personal life from your professional life.

There is no separation.

Mixing the two, especially on social networking sites, can have dire consequences...dire consequences...dire...

dire = terrible, awful, dismal

Maybe it's the school I work for...doesn't sound quite right, but, if I insist on separating personal life from professional life my role as teacher = dire.

RULES OF THE SAME

The 1st rule of Teaching is:

You do not teach the way you were taught.

The 2nd rule of Teaching is:

You DO NOT teach the way you were taught!

3rd rule of Teaching:

If students yell "fight!", gather in a rugby huddle while changing classes, or record hallway brutality with their cell phones, a fight is in progress...engage at your own risk.

4th rule:

Sometimes it will be easier to ask forgiveness, than to ask for permission.

5th rule:

One plight at a time.

6th rule:

Teaching is a bare knuckle operation. No shyness. No superficial pretense. No weapons.

7th rule:

Grading and lesson planning will go on as long as it has to.

And the 8th and final rule:

If this is your first year teaching, you have to fight.

Somewhere along the spotted line, I forgot the 2 most important Rules of Teaching. I got bogged down in the bullshit...the weekly documentation of lesson plans...submitting grades to the internet in a timely manner...committee meetings...collaborative meetings...coaching a sport I never played... and so on...

Recently however, I've been rediscovering the teacher I once aspired to be.

7:46AM

Unlock the door to Room 300. Grab handle with right hand and pull door towards body. Light switch off. Morning seeping through the window frames. A puddle the size of a Soprano stagnantly sits (hello alliteration) in the middle of my classroom. Sunlight bounces off the floor. Liquid mirror.

Me = What the f...

Light switch on.

Internal Me = Yep. Still there...

Put down my computer bag with no computer (I store my lunch in the front compartment sometimes), drop the papers I haven't finished, and will not finish, grading near my scholastic fishing pole (a.k.a. metal pipe), and pull up a chair in front of the puddle.

Internal Me = Couldn't have come from the ceiling...no water marks...where the h....is there a water trail or anything....no not rea....oh! wait...damn....came from where those radiators used to be.

When I inherited Room 300 it came with two radiators that didn't work. From the way they looked when I moved in, my guess is that students used them as trashcans over the years. Corroding metal boxes stuffed to the brim with candy wrappers, dust, chocolate pieces, and dead cockroaches. You could see the wrappers easy, they were sticking out of the vents.

This past summer the radiators were removed during the abatement. In case you're unfamiliar with that term, my school basically had workers removing carpeting and other materials that might contain asbestos.

After the decorative industrial art was excavated, thin pieces of wood were placed over the unattractive holes left by the radiators, painted, glued and sham wow!...it was all better!

Might as well get some rectangular pieces of construction paper, Elmer's glue, and try to build a brick house.

Sitting in front of my indoor pool, I'm thinking I should probably get a mop...but then again, maybe I shouldn't.

Internal Me = Do I have any change?

Scrounge around my pockets and eventually find 2 dimes and 1 nickel.

Internal Me = ...what the hell...why not...make a wish teacher man...I wish that I would not teach the way I was taught.

Coins flip.

Belly flops into rain water.

Bacteria splash onto my black Chucks.

Internal Me =....hmmm...yep! time to start fighting again!

My reflection dissipates in the wake of government plated coinage, and I can't help but have a Fight Club flashback.

A neu teacher employed by a school district leaves graduate idealism traveling at 60mph. The creativity locks up. The teacher crashes and burns while everyone is watching from a distance.

Now, should he initiate a recall?

Take the number of teachers in the field, A, multiply by the probable rate of failure, B, multiply by the average educator attrition rate, C.

A times B times C equals X.

If X is less than the cost of a recall, he won't do one.

Which school district do you work for?

A major one.

CANNABIS

Ryan Cannabis Neumann

What'd you just say?

Andre = Nothin...(shrugs his shoulders and smirks a little) Ryan Lund Neumann...what'd you think I said?

Andre is a soon-to-be graduating senior I've gotten to know pretty well over the past two years.

Me = Mmmmm...Hmmmm...

Andre = What?....he he...............Cannabis....

5:00PM

Leaving school. Andre's been hanging out in Room 300 since 4:00PM...nothing better to do I guess, but right now, we're walking out of the school....away from the realm that is 300.

Me = Where'd you park?

Andre = Over by you in the back corner...why do you park all the way over there anyway...just like the exercise or somethin?

Me = Nah man, that's the spot I was assigned...been that way for 3 years. You'd think by now I'd get upgraded to teacher status and park with the rest of my co-workers....guess not though. Student for l-i-f-e!

Andre = Ha ha!

Momentary silence as we continue walking to our respective vehicles.

Andre = Neumann cannabis Neumann Neumann cannabis cannabis..ha ha...that's gonna be your new nickname...cannabis...

Me = That doesn't even make sense man...you know I don't do that stuff...if anything, it would be more appropriate for you.

Andre = Nope! Ha ha ha...Ryan Cannabis Neumann...Neumann Neumann Neumann cannabis ya see, you can hardly even notice...neumann cannabis neumann cann....

Me = (laughing a little but trying not to show it) You know talking is a highly overrated commodity...wish I could just go a whole school day without talking to anyone.

Andre = How would you teach your classes?

Me = (shoulder shrug)...ummm, I don't know...pre-made signs?

Andre hops in the Pontiac he recently brought back from Alabama. This particular sedan has been giving him trouble ever since he brought it back; nearly 4 weeks ago. He knows a little about cars and thinks the engine is on its way out. Apparently, whenever he stops at a light, the car shuts down on him.

Me = Be careful man...ya know like, take er easy and what not.

Andre = Planning on it Neumann...I mean cannabis..shit!...I forgot already...ha ha!

Me = ...too much cannabis?

The '97 Pontiac takes a minute to turn over, but eventually it rattles a low roar and Andre idles away.

You're crazy.

Mellman's words echo from ear to ear.

There's only two male teachers in the English Department at my school. Mellman represents the other 50%. Aside from the fact that I find him to be hilarious...he's also great about speaking his mind. He just kind of says it...whatever it happens to be...without reservation...and I find that to be pretty damn awesome because the only time I manage to speak unfiltered, without inhibitions, is when I'm drunk or pissed off..or both.

Mellman = You're crazy.

He's talking about my previous story, Comatose.

We spoke briefly in the hall before 1st block began. I get where he's coming from...it's more of a concerned/worried, "You're crazy."

He's right though...as weird as it sounds...I kinda forget that my desire to be this unorthodoxly effective teacher puts a strain on other, more important, facets of my life.

Engine turns over.

5:10PM.

Internal Me = You are crazy....I am crazy...What the hell am I still doing here?...Go home and be with Mar...moron... seriously!?...you wanna be another marriage that didn't work out?...another divorce statistic...Ryan, you've seen Freedom Writers...you know what happens there...don't be that guy...Mara gets off work at 5:30PM.

Gas pedal down. Go.

5 miles into my drive home momentum comes to an unusual halt. A car has its hazard lights on and is parked in the middle lane of a road that doesn't take kindly to mishaps.

Damn it.

So much for getting home early.

Cars begin to weave around the wounded vehicle. Within a minute, I'm right behind the Pontiac with its hazard lights on...Pontiac...wait a sec!...shi...that's Andre!

Within seconds my car is in Park, emergency brake On, door op...almost open...moving vehicle almost removes door... car door (pause to look) open.

Andre sees me from his rear view mirror, waves, and rolls down his driver's side window. As I'm walking to his window, a car pulls up beside me, next to Andre and asks if I'm trying to push the car out of the way.

I say, "yes," and the man pulls his car off to the side, gets out, and helps me push Andre's car to a parking lot nearby. We shake hands and he proceeds with his life.

I remove my car from the middle of the road and drive over to Andre's.

Andre = What should I write?

Me = Ummm...contact number...uh, what 'had' happened...when you'll be back to pick up your car...and...how bout your name.

Andre = Good thinkin...you have a pencil?

Grab a pencil from my car, Andre writes two notes (one for the front and back dash), grabs his stuff and hops in my car.

Me = Still staying at the same place?

Andre = Yep.

Me = Alrighty then.

Andre lives out of district...like...waaayyyyy out of district. By the time we get to his grandma's place...we're pretty close to the Atlanta airport.

I know the route so well I don't even have to ask for directions.

Me = Well alright sir, here ya go.

Andre = Thanks for the ride Neumann...didn't know which way you were headed when we were leaving school...guess I got lucky.

Me = No worries man, thought I'd stay back a ways just in case...wasn't too sure about your car...guess I was right.

Andre = Ha ha!..yeah, well, see ya. (door closes)

He says something but I can't hear him because the doors are closed...obviously.

Roll down the window.

Andre = Cannabis...ha ha!

Me = Whatever dude...see ya tomorrow.

Andre = See ya!...Oh and Neumann..thanks!

I drive away and check the time.

6:00 PM.

Shit.

CATAWAMPUS

Writing is a solitary existence. Do you exist today?

The mirror in my bathroom is one of those medicine cabinet deals...so like, mirror swings open to the left and reveals storage space for toothpaste, wedding ring, and uh, notes.

About a year ago I had a couple leftover index cards from some sort of abstract class assignment that I don't remember because I didn't write it down and anyway, was feeling inspirational...so I wrote myself a note and taped the resulting words to the inside of my medicine cabinet.

Writing is a solitary existence. Do you exist today?

The idea was pretty simple...get motivated to start writing again.

It took a bit...

For the longest time, it was just another something I read quickly but didn't take time to think about...or really, to even look at.

Do you exist today?

No...Not yet.

4:00AM

Today, Eye tired.

Don't even remember turning the alarm OFF.

5:21AM

Damn.

Monday mornings it's hard to tell who's gonna greet me in the mirror.

Light = ON.

Broken glasses secured by paper clips and scotch tape = ON.

Mirror closed.

Internal me = (one eye open...light blinding) Why...the..f...am I awake?

Mirror open.

Writing is a solitary existence.

Mirror closed.

Internal me = What the hell are you looking at sunshine? Gonna change the world today?..huh?...make a difference? ...inspire .hmmm?...Nope...you're gonna go teach...now I know you get those things confused Ryan, but you're just a teacher...remember?

Mirror open.

Do you exist today?

Mirror closed. Contacts = IN.
Internal me = I don't...feeeell like a teacher.

Mirror open.

Do you exist?

I can do this...Ryan, yes, yes...you can do this...you know you have a good time once you get to school. You like your classes. You're starting to enjoy your job again... It's just the whole getting there part...getting there...GET THERE MAN! Glass = half full, carpe diem and all that bubbly crap...well, it's not crap...you're just not fully awake yet...not awake....

I am catawampus.

cat-a-wam-pus

[kat-uh-wom-puh s]

-adjective

1. askew; awry.

2. positioned diagonally; cater-cornered.

-adverb

3. diagonally; obliquely.

Neumann became impatient, and drove catawampus across the interstate.

Drive from Downtown Atlanta to my school = 24 minutes.

Distance from Downtown Atlanta to my school = 20 miles.

By the time I go from being ITP (inside-the-perimeter) to OTP (outside-the-perimeter) I start losing my nerve.

The ITP to OTP transition takes place approximately 4 to 5 miles into commuter carnage.

Catawampus driving tendencies take place around mile 10.

Toyota recalled more than 2,000,000 vehicles because of a reoccurring malfunction...the gas pedal would stick; thus, driving momentum would not...um...decrease.

I remember this little facet while driving catawampus across I-20.

Smashing down on the gas pedal to bypass an 18-wheeler, lawn maintenance truck, and a Pontiac Aztec (the ugliest car ever made)...more often than not, it is worth the risk.

Pull in student parking lot. Park. Leave the Matrix.

Walking through the student parking lot I'm still not there...

Still not a teacher...

...but I suppose I'm the only one who knows.

Enter school. Enter mailroom. Enter Clock-In ID number:

020310

Clock-In Time = 7:50AM

We're only required to Clock-In.

Clock-Out...trivial matter of an equally forgettable nature.

Clock-Out Time =

Exit mailroom. Enter hallway. Enter stairwell. Ascend stairs.

Exit stairwell. A Jansport backpack hangs on the handle to Room 300.

It's D Bo's pack.

I lift the weathered backpack off the handle, unlock the door, and walk D Bo's belongings to his usual seat. It's a small indication of trust.

D Bo is nowhere in sight but he knows I'll take care of his belongings for him.

On Monday mornings, this is how I become a teacher.

Simple gestures of an understood respect...or if nothing else, an understood responsibility.

Exist...by the time I enter Room 300, it's no longer a question; existence is an absolute must.

SUPERMAN

The lights are off and no one's home. Superman's room is empty...he's still bowling.

Today is Wednesday. Bowling is on Wednesday. For as long as I can remember, bowling has always been on Wednesdays.

Got here a little early...it's 5:00PM.

Let's rewind a bit.

Monthly faculty meeting started promptly at 3:45PM.

February focus = PAI

PAI = Performance Assessment Instrument (Teacher Evaluation)

Cue PAI slideshow. Picture of essential learning questions written on dry erase board. Next slide. Picture of learning standards splattered on white walls with multi-colored border secured by staples...did I mention the border has ruffles?

It has ruffles. Next slide.

Picture of students learning...

Picture 4 students with their heads down, diligently at work, consumed by the task at hand (book work or something),writing utensils feverishly filling in the blanks, desks linearly aligned...smiles on their faces, calm as Hindu cows.

Next slide.

Picture 100+ teachers sitting in an auditorium 20 minutes after the official school day has ended.

Next slide.

Picture me staring at the clock. Next slide.

I try not to bring pens or paper with me to meetings anymore because I end up drawing. Depending on the level of engagement, this can be a good or bad thing. Sometimes I draw my notes. Other times, I draw the places I'd rather be. Last couple of meetings the vibe has been...ummm, a little downtrodden...I found myself drawing escape routes.

Picture me standing up in a seated auditorium. Next slide.

Picture me excusing myself...picture me leaving...evacuating.

End slideshow. Cue ignition.

The 20 mile drive from West Egg to East Egg takes about 45 minutes.

There isn't a direct route. Lots of stoplights. Plenty of time for flashbacks.

Drive from the high school I am a teacher at to the high school I was a student at. Propel past student athletes jogging on the sidewalk outside the neighborhood I grew up in; training for Lacrosse season. Every once and awhile I imagine life as it would have been through a different choice...if I had said "yes" to teaching where I was taught, and "no" to teaching in a world unfamiliar to me.

A momentary abstraction...I know I made the right choice, but I guess that can't stop a guy from thinking, what if?

Park in front of 3607. Punch press the garage code and let myself in. Mom and Erik are still at Bowling. Dad is traveling. Kali is in Portland. Mara is at work. Can't remember the last time it was just me here.

Home alone.

The lights are off and no one's home. Open the fridge. See beer...

Grab a Coke Zero and do a quick walk of the house. Can't get over the quiet.

Superman's room is empty. I push the door open a little to see if Erik's got any new posters or movies spread out on the end of his bed in perfect horizontal lines. He's got so much stuff I can't tell. Think about browsing his movie collection in case there's anything I haven't seen but stop myself...I'll wait til they get home. Pull the door back to where I think it was before I pushed. I'm sure he'll notice anyway.

Erik's funny...he likes all his stuff in a very particular way...his way...and he can tell if anything has been moved or adjusted...even if it's only the slightest of sleights...he can tell.

Everything in its right place.

Walk down the hallway to the bonus room. Mom's got this desk with a glass top near one of the windows. There's all these pictures pressed between the glass and desk...pictures of family, pictures of people who've passed away, pictures of us from when we were younger...

There's this one picture of Erik from when we were in kindergarten; we had one of those pre-K graduation things...got a paper diploma and all that. In the picture Erik's holding his diploma with this sly look on his face...like he's happy, but laughing to himself too...like he's in on some inside joke only he knows about.

Must have been windy that day cause his shaggy brown hair is all blown to one side.

Lay down on the coach. Glance back in the direction of the narrow hallway. Fading afternoon light illuminates the bedroom doorways. Everything else washes out. Maroon paint fades into the shadows. Kryptonite knocks me out.

Power nap.

You should tell em that one story about your brother Mr. Neumann...

...which one?...

I look over to Beth and she's got this knowing smile on her face. Instantly, I know which story she wants me to tell.

Beth = You know...the one when you're walking home from school.

Me = Ohhhh right...ummm...yeah, I don't know...I'm not sure if they want to hear that story...

Students sense the potential for wasted instructional time and zero in on the target...me.

Class= Story?...what story?...why don't you wanna tell it Mr. Neumann?....what had happened....yeah Neumann....now you gotta tell us...that's not fair...come on Lund....tell it! tell it! story!...

Me = ...Alllrriigghhhttt...I need everyone to listen though.

Class = Silence.

Me = So, I've told you guys a little about my brother right? (class = yes)

Me = Alright...well, this one time, when me and Erik were still in high school...I was like, a sophomore or something...we would walk to and from school every day because we lived so close. In the morning, me and Erik would usually just walk by ourselves but in the afternoon, some of my friends would walk back with us...so, this one afternoon, me and Erik were going back and forth, you know, arguing the way brothers do and what not...oh! but here's what you need to know about Erik...he'll either be IN talking mode OR he WILL NOT be in talking mode when we would be walking home from school...so, this one afternoon, he was not in talking mode because my friends were walking with us and Erik can be a little shy and anyway, Erik and I are arguing to the point where he decides to spit on me and push me off the sidewalk where cars are driving by....so I'm like, in total disbelief, like totally WTF, not mention I almost get hit by a car so I get back on the sidewalk and we continue to argue...meanwhile ya know, my friends are all cracking up because this is high quality entertainment for teenage boys...and then, Erik tries to spit on me again only this time he misses...and I'm like, hell no...so I grab this stick I see on the ground and throw it at Erik, right...you know, like that's my shot at getting him back for spitting on me and pushing off the sidewalk.

Me = So now, picture this...it's the first few weeks of the semester just like it is now for you guys...and this girl who, unknown to me, is in like, my social studies class and her mom picks her up from school and they're driving home and this girl looks out her window and sees this boy throwing a stick at another boy who has Down Syndrome...

Class = Fully attentive

Me = Now fast forward to the next day of school. I walk in to my social studies class, sit down, minding my own business and what not, and I overhear this girl behind me talking about this horrible thing she saw some jerk do after school yesterday...apparently, this guy was picking on a handicapped kid...throwing a stick at this poor innocent kid as he's walking home from school.

Me = So, I overhear all of this and turn around and say something likeI...

"ummm...that (pause) story you're talking about. Sorry, but, I think that boy you're talking about is me."

Girl (Roseann) = Yeah! I knew it was you all along. You're an asshole!!

The door to 3607 slams shut. The lights are on and some one's home.

BABY'S MAMA

She took her.

Internal Me = ...uh...took her took her...took....her....I don't know what he's talking about...I don't know what you're talking about, man.

Me = Took? Her? I don't know what you're talking about, man.

Joseph = (forceful shrug of shoulders)...you know, my little girl.

Me = Ohhhh!..what!?! Who?

Joseph = My baby's mama (yes, he really said that)

Me = When?

Joseph = Over the weekend...She just came over and took her when I wasn't home.

Internal Me = Confused.

Me = Huh?...What do you mean?...How could she just come over and....

Joseph = (helpless shrug of shoulders)...Idonknow.

Me = Are you OK?

Joseph = No.

2 minute bell rings. 120 seconds until the next class begins. Joseph and I are standing in the hallway with a mobile audience.

Me = Wellll...wait a sec, come in here for a minute.

We walk into Room 300 where, at least for the moment, no one else is.

Me = Sooo...OK, girl, gone, you, not OK...and...go.

Joseph = Idonknow...Idonknow what to do...I mean, California is way too far away. I don't have the money to go out there and get er back.

Me = California? She lives in California?...your bab..(almost said it)...the mother of your child lives in California...came all the way to Georgia just to take your (I use hand motions to suggest the baby belonging to the both of them but it really just looks like I'm clawing air) baby while you weren't around and then...she leaves. Do your parents know about this?

Joseph = Yep.

How much do you think land costs in Mexico?

Internal Me = WTF

Andre = Neumann! D'ya hear me? Land! How much do you think it costs in Mexico?

While attempting to answer Andre's question Joseph silently exits Room 300. Things like this happen every day. That is to say, conversations that really need to be, uh, conversated, don't because of interruptions.

Me = I. have. absolutely. no. idea..

Questions get interrupted by other questions.

Neumann! Why is the word number abbreviated with the letters N and O?...ya know, like No.?

Why are you a hobo Neumann?

What do you teach?

Did you get my text?

Did you get my email?

Lund! Why isn't my drawing on the wall?

Mr. Neumann, if Mario was in it for the Princess, what was Luigi in it for?

What's my grade?

What are we doing today?

Are you any good at math?...I didn't do my homework?

How old are you?...really?...that old?

Do you always wear Converse?

When are you going to shave?

I try my best to answer every question. I want to answer every question. Ya see, the thing is, I'll take students...random students...students I don't know...won't even remember tomorrow....and I'll try to answer their questions because they're willing to come up and ask me a question.

I don't have 100% participation in the classes I teach. I mean, there's some...I have some voluntary diatribe but, I also have blank stares and timid afterthoughts.

Randomness...questions about land in Mexico or questions based on speculation...like inquiries about where I met my wife, if I was really almost fired (No), or if I actually threw a kid's cell phone across a room and into a radiator (Yes)...questions like that drive the dull away.

But it's the interrupted conversations that make me worry...broken moments of vulnerability...statements like, I'm done with this school...I'm OK (when obviously he or she is not OK)...I don't think I'm going to graduate...OR...she took her..

AN ALL NIGHT THING

Heart. Punching. Chest. From. Inside. Out.

Sweating...slouching upright in bed...where's Mara?

Where are my glasses?...Why does it feel like I've been injected with Red Bull?...What time is it?

9:21AM...Sunday

Why the hell am I awake?

Mind not working correctly. Fragmented action items pummel my frontal lobe like collapsing Jenga pieces on a coffee table.

Teacher Observation week. Mara's Mom. Surgery. Piedmont. Mara. 6 Week Grades. Parent Phone Calls. Bowling. Superbowl. Mara. Lesson Plans. Special Education Certification Tests. Mara, Laundry, LAUNDRY, boo, laundry.

Where to start?

Stagger out of bedroom visionless. Self inflict sight.

Throw first batch of laundry in the wash: whites, colors, darks, reds, motivation, flannel shirts, focus, jeans, towels; no discrimination.

Tired. Lay down on chase lounge. Mara's relaxing on the couch. Eyes close.

Wake up at 12:15PM with absolutely nothing accomplished...but I feeeell rested.

Need more time. Do the math in my head...
bowling + superbowl party + drive time = 7 to 9 hours...that puts us back home between 9PM and 11PM at which point I will have done...nothing for school.

Hmmm...all nighter?

Finish inserting grades into computer database around midnight.

Laundry done by 2AM.

Exercise and work on lesson plans from 2:01AM to 3:35AM.

Lay down in bed with Mara until 4:30ish. Can't sleep; neither can Mara. She gets out of bed at 4AM and starts getting ready.

Stare at the ceiling for another 3o minutes and go back to work...finish lesson plans and what not.

Mara leaves for the hospital slightly before 5:30AM. She's headed towards Piedmont to wish her mom well before surgery...don't even know if this makes sense, but...I can't seem to figure out who I'm worried about more at this point...Mara or her mom.

Run 4 miles on the residential treadmill located on the 2nd floor of my gentrified world. Have no idea where the energy is coming from...it's 6AM.

Clock-in time at school = 7:48 and big brother is watching...

Nearing the 20 hour mark. 8:15AM...time to teach.
Got everything ready already...lesson plans...clearly labeled
folder...just in case.

3:25PM...no observation today...damn...guess that's what they meant
by "unannounced".

Drive home. Wait for Mara to get off work. Make her some food. Ride
to the hospital. All is well :) ...relief!

10:00PM = 34 hours of awakeness and I feeellll...fine...weird...why the
hell am I awake?

10:15PM = Asleep.

Out. Inside. From. Chest. Punching. Heart.

SHOW ME LITTLE SHAME

It ain e'en dat serious brah, fa real...u jus nee da relax wit all dat.

Internal Me = Listen to him Ryan. He's right...be calm.

Me = I know...brah...for real...so why don't you just relax with the candy wrappers...still got some people taking the test (I point)...like the person right behind you...for instance.

Meet Shaun. I just did. Today is Shaun's first day of school. Actually, today is Shaun's first day of school for the entire 2009 – 2010 school year.

Shaun = I know. I gotch u...s'what I'm sayin...relax...u id'nt e'en nee da say all dat.

Internal Me = Enunciate your fuuuuhhh...fricking words man. Seriously, Ryan, don't do it...he's testng you...he wants to see if he can get a rise out of you...he's probably just pissed off he's here and wants you to feel the same way.

Me = I know I did not need to say all that. But I did. Please forgive me.

Shaun's backpack is a drawstring shoe bag...it's full of candy. And just to be clear, he doesn't have a bag full of candy for some insanely sweet tooth...Shaun has a bag full of candy so he can sell to fellow students.

Shaun continues to empty the contents of his bag onto the desktop. The 23 other students comprising this particular 2nd block class remain quiet. They know the drill.

3 students are still completing the county mandated practice test I've been instructed to administer. Everyone is to remain quiet until all tests have been completed...for the illusion of a peaceful testing environment...so that no child may be left behind.

Shaun sits at his desk wrestling plastic Starburst wrappers out of his shoe bag; blissfully unaware that he has the attention of the entire class.

I try the silent motioning thing...ya know, get his attention with some hand gestures...make the shhhh sign...and hope for the best. I do this a couple times to no avail.

Finally, I say, "Dude...you need to give the candy wrappers a rest."

The fun begins.

Shaun = I'm doin sumpin...u don nee da go yellin an all dat.

Me = I wasn't yelling. Promise. You would know if I was.

Shaun = I'm tellin ya man...ya nee da quit all dat...befo I have to go an put cha ya in yor place...aight?

Internal Me = You've got to be fucking kidding me.

Me = Nah man, that's not aight...actually, I need to speak with you out in the hallway for a second.

Shaun = Well shit...I ain gettin up...I get up an imight have to put chu in yor place.

Sometimes I get really fucking tired of repetition.

Me = Actually, that would be perfect...because, my place is right out here (motion to the hallway) in the hallway. Do you think you could help me? Why don't cha follow me? Here...yeah...real quick...it'll only take a sec.

I start walking towards the door...towards the hallway where, for the first time in a long time, I'm not entirely sure what's going to happen next.

I feel like destroying something beautiful.

I stand waiting by the open exit that is Room 300.

Shaun = Hope u don min waitin...cuz I ain rushin fa nobody.

Me = Oh no man, that's fine. Take your time, I mean, I do have all day.

Some of the students in class are laughing...I don't know if it's at me or Shaun because I refuse to break eye contact with Shaun. I don't even think I'm blinking at this point.

Shaun = I'm so sick of this lame shit...fucking teachers...(insert unintelligible mumbles for another 2 or 3 fragments)

There's this scene in the Bourne Ultimatum where Matt Damon is jumping from roof to roof in some third world country. Eventually, he jumps through a window to save the damsel in distress (Julia Styles) and ends up in an intense altercation with some assassin. At one point, Matt Damon hits his enemy in the face with a book and proceeds to beat him senselessly with said book...punching the book which in turn, punches the enemy in the face. This scene comes to mind as Shaun says, "...fucking teachers."

Internal Me = Don't cuss. You're going to cuss aren't you? Yep, you are...well...shit, Ryan, go head, get it over with.

Me = Ya know you're right Shaun. I completely agree. This shit is pretty fucking lame. Thank you for getting up out of your seat though...I really appreciate it.

Trail him into the hall. He's about 4 steps ahead of me.

Shaun = in the hallway. Me = standing in the doorway. He looks at me. I look at him.

Me = Thank you. Welcome to your place. Peace.

I shut the door.

Class = disbelief about the happenings.

My hand is on the door handle. Waiting for Shaun to make the attempt at reentry.

Door pulls out. I pull back in for a second and then give a little.

Immediately I hear him.

Shaun = You idn't e'en nee dado all dat. Lemme get my stuff man.

Me = (hand on door handle...blocking Shaun from reentering class). Nah man, it's cool...I got it...I'll get your stuff.

He stays. Hand him his stuff. Close door. Need time to think.

Think. Think...thinking. Open door. Exit class. Close door.
Staring at the ground trying to find the words. Shaun's looking down the extensive hallway with a song blaring from the speakers on his cell phone.

Me = So uhhh...what's the problem?

Shaun = Problem?...I ain got no problm...u da one wit da problm.

Me = Ooookkkk...welll, do you want to be here?

Shaun = If I didn wanna be here, I wouldn be here...nobody tells me wat ta do.

Me = Ok well, I mean, do you like being here?...are you getting anything out of being here?

Shaun = I on't know...Im gonna do wat I wanna do...don't matter if you say do this or don do this.

Me = ...Alright...well, do you want to come back to class?

Shaun = It don madder to me. You go head and do wat you was gonna do...I'm chillin.

Me = ...Hmmm...wellll....how bout this. Choice is yours...we don't have too much time left in class but...if you would like to come back in and join us...you are more than welcome to...if not, that's fine too...you can just chill out here.

Shaun = (thinkng for a moment)...I'll chill out here.

Me = Ok...well if you change your mind, the door is unlocked.

Shaun = Aight

Me = Haaa...aight.

Close door. Class ends. Shaun does not reenter. Planning period begins. Should probably check email. Not right now. Insert headphones. Press Play. Injected:

Too much left to say...never wanted it that way...now you wake up wondering why your life is tumbling into...nothing left to say.

JUST BREATHE

Wednesday *(Yesterday)-**February 10, 2010***

10:13AM

From: Guidance Counselor

To: Neumann, Ryan; Stevens, Perry

Good Morning,

Shaun Cowart enrolled this morning and has been placed in one of your classes. There are no transfer grades, so he will be responsible for all work so far this semester if he is to earn full credit.

Thanks.

Guidance Counselor

Wednesday (Yesterday)-February 10, 2010

10:19 AM

From: Perry Stevens

To: Guidance Counselor; Neumann, Ryan

Ma'am,

I spoke to Shaun this morning and he made it very clear to me that he has little to no desire to be enrolled in school. However, he seems like a very bright young man. Is there any contact info for his parents so I can speak with them as soon as possible to hopefully get him started on the right track? I would like to do a positive contact prior to any negative issues that may arise.

Respectfully,

Perry Stevens

Too bad I didn't read these emails until after I met Shaun.

Let me give you a quick breakdown of my...yesterday

1st Block...

4 county police officers + 1 drug dog + 1 administrator + Room 300 = Search Party!

2nd Block...

Introducing Shaun Cowart

3rd Block...

Planning...listen to teachers complain about this and that...our job as glorified babysitters...I need a drink...horrible students...bad parents...merit pay...I could really use a drink...furlough days...and on and on.

4th Block...

Finally got my unannounced observation...it was horrible...ummm yeah, anything that could go wrong...did...enough said.

When I'm stressed out I go to sleep super early. My body just kind of shuts down. Mara knows this. Guess it's my way of escaping reality...escaping a professional lifestyle that can be ridiculously demoralizing and undeniably rewarding all at once.

Mara had an architecture reunion last night (Wednesday).

I was asleep on the couch at 7:30PM.

Thursday (Today)-February 11, 2010

8:18AM

From: Ryan Neumann

To: Guidance Counselor

Do you have any information on Shaun?....like where he's coming from?...schools?...family?

Thursday (Today)-February 11, 2010

9:37AM

From: Guidance Counselor

To: Neumann, Ryan

He has not been in school since May. He attended County West Middle School. His plan was to go to job corp, but it did not work out for him.

Email isn't always the most effective means of communication.

2nd block begins. Shaun is nowhere to be found.

I am relief.

Suddenly I hear an oh so familiar tapping...

Door opens. It's Shaun!

What a relief.

Me = Morning sir.

Shaun = Wad up.

Me = Got a pass?

Shaun = Nah.

Me = Well I can't let you in if you don't have a pass, man.

Shaun = Well I ain got a pass an I ain gettin a tardy slip so I'll jus be out here in my place chillin.

Internal Me = Great.

Me = Great.

Shaun politely closes the door solidifying the barrier between himself and us.

Internal Me = Breathe Ryan...Just Breathe...what's the best way to approach the situation?

Open Room 300. Step outside. Close Room 300. Deja Vu.

Me = Alright man, is today going to be like yesterday?

Shaun= Only gonna be like yesterday if u wan it to be.

I am speechless. He's absolutely right...do I want today to be like yesterday?...No!...definitely not.

One of the first rules I remember my irrefutably awesome department chair (Cainage) teaching me, and one that Shaun is already well aware of, is a problem is I've forgotten. Some things you just have to drop...doesn't matter if it's petty or profound...teaching the kids...teaching the students that I teach, that we teach...requires an acquired short term memory. Can't get bogged down in trivial wrongdoings...especially when school is an escape for many of the students enrolled in the public institutions around here. Sure, they may not be willing to admit it, but it's true. You can see it on their faces.

Why am I getting so bent out of shape? Why can't I let things slide as easily as I used too. Why am I feeling pissed off more often than not?..It's not because of Shaun...I don't even know Shaun.

Me = You're right man. You wanna come back to class?

Shaun = Yea...a'd be straight.

Me = Alright cool, but first...why were you late to class?

Shaun = Well, seein how its my secund day here...dis a pretty big school an I wadn't quite sure how da get back here.

Man I feel like an ass.

Me = (I open the door) after you, sir.

Shaun = Thanks

SHUT THE F UP

FRIDAY

From: Jacquelyn Montgomery

To: Neumann, Ryan

Subject: incident in class

2/26/2010

2:32 PM

Hi Ryan,

I had to follow up with a few of your students regarding a minor incident in your classroom while you were at your duty post during first block class change. It appears that Kevin and Myriam indulged in "horse play" that resulted in Myriam's arm being compromised. The parent is at the hospital at this time waiting to hear the outcome of the harm that may have been inflicted.

One student reported that Myriam said "Shut the F Up" to another student and then asked you (Neumann) to go and see the nurse.

Did you hear anything like this from Myriam?

Thank you so much for your help!

The academic school day, for students, ends at 3:25PM.

On Fridays, at 3:25:01, the weekend officially begins for both students and teachers. It would be wise to disregard those teachers who have their planning period during the last, regularly scheduled, class of the day. More than likely, those teachers are MIA.

Protocol dictates an 8AM to 4PM workday.

From: Ryan Neumann

To: Montgomery, Jacquelyn

Subject: Re: incident in class

2/26/2010

3:49 PM

Good Afternoon Ms. Montgomery,

Yes, I did hear Myriam say that exact phrase...Shut the F Up. However, there is, or was, a gap between that phrase and Myriam going to the nurse. I will write a more detailed account of the class happenings and email another response ASAP.

From: Jacquelyn Montgomery

To: Neumann, Ryan

Subject: Re: re: incident in class

2/26/2010

5:04 PM

Thank you!

SATURDAY...blink...SUNDAY...hold your breath...looks like somebody's got a case of the...

MONDAY

From: Jacquelyn Montgomery

To: Neumann, Ryan

Subject: Re: re: really: incident in class

3/1/2010

10: 30 AM

Do you have the statement?

Internal Me = No. I'm trying to teach...but hell, let me drop everything to write an accident report for an accident I didn't see.

Me =Mouse click...next message.

3/1/2010

10: 51 AM

I just wanted to let you know that the mother of Myriam is thinking of charging the male student with assault. I told her that it was a mutual horseplay and that the school was not going to pursue that route.

I do need a very accurate statement form (from) you.

Thank you.

Me = Still teaching…

11:00AM

Subject: Please Move

Myriam and Kevin away from each other

Internal Me =…like, holy f (don't cuss)…shit, seriously?

RE: SHUT THE F UP

Will you marry me?

Date = 7.10.2007

Place = Stockholm, Sweden

Mara and I were sitting on a park bench facing the water.

She was exhausted...she'd been walking around Stockholm the entire day with her classmates...looking at architecture and sketching in moleskine notebooks.

I voluntarily spent the day alone; walking around the city.

Ring in pocket...the ring, not having left my pocket in nearly 5 days.

Meandered for hours. Finally came across this park bordering a body of water...near this place called Riddarfjardens Marina.
It's just a few blocks down from where the Nobel Prize is dished out every year.

Everything was green. An abundance of trees, grass...tall blades of life jutting out everywhere water met land.

Internal Me = This is it.

Even though it was July, the weather was still kind of chilly. I was just hoping it wouldn't rain.

The afternoon turned out to be sunny although it began breezy and was cloudy for quite sometime; I'd say mid 50's, low 60's...but eventually, sunlight prevailed.

We're sitting on this park bench later that evening. The sun is melting. Orange and red hues drip behind the shadowy buildings in the distance. Mara's so tired she's not making sense...singing the chorus to some Shakira song in an unintelligible mumble.

I fumble around in my pockets like I have something for her. A small gift perhaps...cookies, a drawing, a note...

Come up empty handed. Sitting on the park bench. Mara to my right. I lean over to ask her something...speaking at a volume that only she would be able to hear...voicing a question that was only ever meant for her:

Will you marry me?

Instantly, Mara perks up. Actually, she jumps...like literally...I'd say she got 2 inches of air...like, no problem at all. Looks at me and says:

Shut the fuck up!...

Internal Me = Hmmm....well, not exactly the answer I was hoping for...

...are you serious?

I start laughing a little. Smile from ear-to-ear.

Me = Yeah.

Guess you can figure out the rest but here's the deal, ever since that day, since Mara said, *Shut the fuck up!*...I've had this image of her ingrained in my head.

So, when Myriam said, "Shut the F Up," to Kevin in class the other day, the first thing that came to mind was Mara.

4:01 PM

3/1/2010

Internal Me = Alright...what'd Ms. Montgomery say?...*I do need a very accurate statement form* (from) *you...*

Beginnith accurism.

From: Neumann, Ryan

To: Jacquelyn Montgomery

INTERNAL ME Subject: Shut the F Up

Subject: Re: re: re: really: Myriam

10:10AM (2nd Block)

From 10:05AM to 10:10AM, I stood beside the open door of Room 300 to greet students and keep an eye on the happenings of the English hallway.

This past Friday (2.26.2010), all students were in class when the tardy bell rang. As soon as the late bell rang, I shut the door and immediately had to address the actions of two young men located next to the doorway. One boy was sitting down at a table while the other was standing and peering through the open backpack of the seated boy.

The boy who was seated periodically brings two backpacks to class. One backpack is full of candy which he attempts to sell to fellow students on a daily basis. The student, who was standing, was examining the contents of the candy backpack to decide what

he wanted to purchase. Upon noticing this, I motioned to the boy that their actions were inappropriate. The boys chose to ignore my warning at which point I confiscated the back pack and directed the two young men to their seats.

Myriam and Kevin were in their usual seats. That is to say, Kevin sits in the row directly behind Myriam.

Class typically begins with CNN Student News. CNN Student News is a 10 minute news broadcast designed specifically for students. Embedded within the episode are student response questions called Shout Outs. These questions encourage students to call out the correct answer to a multiple choice question. Friday's question focused on basketball.

As each answer choice resonated through the classroom speakers, Kevin would say basketball loud enough for myself and the students around him to hear his verbalization.

Example:...is the correct answer A. hockey (Kevin = basketball!) B. soccer (Kevin = basketball!) C. basketball (Kevin = basketball) or D. football (Kevin = basketball!)

Having had enough of Kevin's outbursts, Myriam told Kevin to SHUT THE F— UP!

My initial reaction was to walk up to where Kevin was sitting, lean over and say something to the effect of, "hey man, you need to relax with the outbursts...I know you're just playing around, but ya know, not everyone is down with that."

I then stood up and asked Myriam if I could speak to her in the hallway.

She was more than obliging, and as I shut the door to the classroom, Myriam and I had a brief discussion about what just happened. I told her she can't be dropping F-bombs whenever she gets frustrated, but at the same time, I can't control what Kevin will and will not do. I told Myriam that if Kevin should start calling out random answers for the heck of it, again, that I would definitely be speaking with him. Myriam apologized and told me that she knew she shouldn't be saying that in class, and that she wouldn't say it again...she was just frustrated. I reassured her that I would speak with Kevin when necessary and asked if there was anything else I could do.

She said no and we reentered the classroom. From what I recall, and I'll admit my memory is a bit hazy here, we managed to watch the rest of CNN Student News. I could have sworn Myriam asked to go to the nurse after the CNN Student News episode was over. I did not ask Myriam why she needed to go to the nurse. I do not receive that many requests for female students to go to the nurse, but past experiences (student going into labor during class) have taught me to say yes without asking too many questions. Perhaps that is a fault of my own, but unless the student has a history of leaving class, skipping class, or unexcused behavior, I have no problems saying yes to a nurse request.

Myriam left for the nurse and I proceeded with class. Several minutes later, I am unsure of the actual time, Myriam came back and showed me a note that said she was checking out. She did seem a little upset. I asked her if she needed anything but don't think that registered with her. Myriam took a minute to gather her things and then left class. Before leaving, I believe she did say something to another student about a class they had later on in the day.

Throughout that entire time, Kevin was acting as he always does in class....relatively relaxed but always happy to talk if someone has a question or wants to talk to him.

Towards the end of class 2 administrators visited class to inform me of the situation. I was utterly perplexed as to how a student could have gotten her arm slammed in the door to Room 300 as I routinely stand by the door during class changes. I was trying to figure out how I could have been so absent-minded as to miss something like that happening.

The administrators briefly spoke to my second block class asking if anyone knew anything about a young lady getting her arm slammed in the doorway. Class was quiet. No one knew anything and for the most part, everyone looked clueless. However, I did notice that Kevin had a slightly disgruntled look on his face and shifted in his chair a bit.

After the administrators left, I addressed the class. I asked that if there really was or is someone who knew what may have happened to Myriam, but felt uncomfortable raising their hand or hands, would those people please write an anonymous note and leave it in the classroom on their way out the door.

Class ended and no notes were left.

Alright Ryan, that's enough for today...

Shut the F Up!

BUTTERFLY EFFECT

Portable Electronic (battery operated) Compact Disc Player.

Insert burned CD.

Artist = Rage Against the Machine.

Album = The Battle of Los Angeles.

Song = **Maria.**

"...I am, nothing...no one...nobody...no more..."

August. 2001.

Introspective revelation. Music helps me write.

Boone, North Carolina.

Appalachian State University.

ENG 101 =Introduction to English Composition.

Paper Topic #1 = Definition Paper

My former internal self = ...I really HATE WRITING! Definition paper...seriously?...what the hell am I going to define in 3-5 pages...this guy's a joke...he's not even a real professor...he's aaaa...a what...a TA?....what the f....MLA format...freaking...I thought I was done with all this crap. Definition paper definition paper...I can define whatever I want huh?...great, what shall I define then? Sarcasm? Binge drinking? Oh great, sample topics...skimming skimming...butterfly affect?...butterfly effect?...

-noun

1. A chaotic effect created by something seemingly insignificant.

2. The phenomenon whereby a small change in one part of a complex system can have a large effect somewhere else.

...from the beating of a butterfly's wings in one place causing a tornado in another place.

Close the dictionary and look around.

When I was an undergrad I lived in the library. Always by the windows too...second floor. Quiet Study area. There was this long row of glass the length of the building. Created this amazingly panoramic shot of campus and the mountains in the distance.

I'd bury myself in school work Sunday through Thursday most weeks. But eventually, I'd need a little escape from school work so I'd thumb through some burned CDs, throw one in my little anti-shock portable CD player, and take 5 minutes to escape...look out those windows...at the mountains and just...disappear.

*The butterfly effect is a common trope in fiction when presenting scenarios involving time travel and with "**what if**" scenarios where one storyline diverges at the moment of a seemingly minor event resulting in two significantly different outcomes.*

March. 2010.

OTP (outside-the-perimeter)

At the school I work for, there's this narrow section on the second floor of the Media Center that goes unused much of the day. A long row of windows with partially closed blinds suggest a world beyond the walls of whatever it is I do here.

Frequently, I quarantine myself in this dormant section of the Media Center during my planning period. It reminds me of Boone. I can work on my work...pretend to be sane...and just sort of, escape without actually escaping.

Looking at the day's lesson plan...

*The butterfly effect is a common trope in fiction when presenting scenarios involving time travel and with "**what if**" scenarios where one storyline diverges at the moment of a seemingly minor event resulting in two significantly different outcomes.*

Hmmm...

(later in the day)

Me = Alright guys...so we haven't done a whole lot of...uh...scholastic work as far as writing goes this week...so, I've got some writing prompts for this next part of class.

Insert rolling of eyes...here.

Me = OK...so, all in all, I'm gonna need a full page of writing from you by the end of class today BUT!...you can accomplish this goal in a variety of ways.

Pull on the roll down projector screen to activate the automatic roll-up springs thus unveiling the rarely used dry-erase board.

No roll-up.

Try again.

Again.

Roll-out...

Me = OK, so...We...or, uh, you are playing with "what if" scenarios today.

I step to my left (student right) and point to a list of what ifs.

1. What if 9/11 never happened?

2. What if we (United States) were not in a recession?

Class is quiet...I'd venture to say even intrigued.

3. What if you could....

BAM BAM BAM BAM BAM BAM BAM BAM....

Attentive young minds abruptly swivel their heads to the right.

I pivot to the left.

All eyes focus on the door to Room 300.

Pin-dropping silence.

BAM BAM stops.

Door swings open.

No one is there.

Avert my attention from the empty doorway to the facial expressions of 20 something 9th graders. Curiosity.

Glance back to the left. A boy now stands in the doorway. He's wearing a zip-up hoodie. Face covered in shadows from said hoodie...some students start to giggle...He (Cameron) stands mute; a deviant smirk speaking volumes. Without saying a word, he starts walking towards his usual seat in the front of the classroom.

I walk towards Cameron so as to intercept. Walking at me with no intention of stopping I tell Cameron to turn around.

Me = Turn Around.

We walk out the door to Room 300. Into the hallway.

Close the door to Room 300.

3. What if you could...alter your past?

"...I am, nothing...no one...nobody...no more..."

WRITING TOPIC RESULTS

Write 1 page (MLA format) about 1 or ALL of the following what ifs.

1. What if 9/11 never happened?

2. What if we (United States) were not in recession?

3. What if you could alter your past?

9th Grade lit

Jasmine King

What if I could change my past?

IF I could change my past I would have kept my grades up instead of letting them Fall and let me begin to fail. I would take back my being sick to where I had to get a spinal tap and moved which messed up my legs. I would love to take back things I have said, done, and saw. I would love to get my parents back together and get them to be a happy family again.

Kevin Mosley

march 11, 2010

2nd period

What if you could alter your past?

If I could alter my past it would be alot of things I would change. I would change the way I insult people, and come up with something even more insulting. I would change the things I got myself in trouble for the way I insult people and be ready to insult them. Just kidding around I would really change the way I treated my past girlfriends and friends and do something to get better friends cause those guys were week. lol. But really thow you got to ask yourself if it wasnt for yo past then you wouldn't be the person you are today, like everyone you have flaws but most of the flaws I don't like about me, some people love about me "mostly girls". But really I wouldn't because I like who I am, cocky, good-looking, and funny. Who doesn't like that kind of guy? lol. But it wouldn't matter if I could, I wouldn't alter anything, just try to love everything.

Xavier Black

Neumann

9th Lit

3/11/10

If I could alter the very fabric of time the first thiNg I would do is go back iN time and stop the man who killed my uNcle. After that I would meet both of my graNdfathers siNce they both died before I was borN with my mothers father dyiNg iN the year I was borN. After doiNg that little adventure I would go to the preseNt aNd see how much had chaNged. Hopefully Not much would of happNed siNce I had beeN scewiNg arouNd with the past. If somehow somethiNg bad did happeN I would go to the past to stop myself.

What if I could alter THe Past?

David Jones

Mr. Neumann

9th Grade LIT

3/11/10

If I could alter my past I wold alter quiet a few things. For example I my DaD gave me this gold rope necklace and I let this girl wear it, THen she Lost IT. When I told my Dad he was hurt, he saiD "he woulD never Do THat again," So if I coulD I wouLD have never gave her IT. ALso I Wish I never haD goT expelled from my miDDle School for 7 fights. If I coulD I woulD go Back and Be a BeTTer person and not Fight. If I coulD aLter my Past I WoulD go Back anD not puT Many Bags oF weeD In my Jacket, and BreakIng my moTHers heart When she founD Out, I go Back and make a Smart Decscicision To say no To Dealing Drugs.-only IF I coulD alter my pasT...

Anthony Manero

Mr. Neumann

American Literature

11 March 2010

What if...

If I could alter my past, I may still be in New Orleans, Louisiana. Hopefully, I could stop Hurricane Katrina. It was one of the most traumatizing experiences in my life. I would also change the way I talked around middle school and elementary schools in New Orleans. My actions put me in an uncomfortable position in my life.

Shaun Cowart
March 11, 2010

Mr. Neumann

9th lit.

1) What if 9/11 wouldn't never happend?

Well my opinion if 9/11 never happend so many people would not be hurting from the pain of their loved one dying. Another reason reason is, if 9/11 wouldn't happend so many people wouldn't have opened their eyes to see that the world is full of evil people and things. Also if 9/11 would not have happend we woudn't be in this stupid war.

2) What if we weren't in a recession?

If we weren't in a recession president Obama wouldn't be where he is now. (President of the United States). If we weren't in a recession people would have jobs and they'd be able to provide their family with things they need to survive.

3) What if you could alter your past?

If I could change my past my grandma would still be alive. My uncle Stack would still be here as well.

4) What if you were a different race?

Honestly I wouldn't wanna be a different race.

Demonte Hudson

Mr. Neumann

Block 2

3/11/10

If I was to alter my past...to be honest if I was lucky enough to have that power...I wouldn't change a thing. Its very simple to mess up something by altering the past. I could prevent my birth, stop one of my siblings from ever being born, or breakup my parents. My present is already good, and I don't want to risk changing it.

To me people can be really stupid. Because they never take time to think of the possibilities. For example when most people think of the modern black man they think of the common stereotype. Big, baggy clothes, mostly uses slang terminology, violent, likely to be affiliated with gang activity, probably uses drugs, listens to rap, and doesn't do well at school. But what I hate the most is that people live up to the stereotypes. Take that one kid sitting two rows in front of me (Shaun Cowart). He looks exactly like the stereotypes, practically a spitting image.

Now look at me, I do well in school, barely use slang, don't wear baggy clothes, don't use drugs, listen to rock music from the 60s and I'm a Boy Scout. There are other people in this class who have common sense, like Xavier. He is very good at math. But if I did have a chance to change my race, I'd probably say no because my life wouldn't be different. I would still keep away from drugs, dress properly, do well in school, listen to rock music, and be a Boy Scout.

Derrick Lee

Mr. nuemann

Am lit/4th block

03-11-010

If I was a different race. I would be White, because White almost run the world. White people can bout do anything and get away with it. White people real low down to. They think they batter then every body else. White people don't like for black people to have nothing cause they scare we gone out do them. I want to just know what its like to be white.

OCCUPATIONAL HAZARD

This shit is gay.

Pause.

If my life were a sitcom, I'd have those built-in timeouts like Zach Morris on **Saved by the Bell**...those were sweet.

Rewind 30 seconds and...

Play.

Me = Ok...so, take a second and fold your handout in half...hot dog style.

If I say vertical it's like I'm reciting Shakespeare.

I say hot dog, I say hamburger...we all happy.

Each student has a photocopied handout with a hand drawn butterfly on one side that I didn't draw because for the most part, I can't stand...no wait...I hate drawing at this point in my life.

Guess it's a good thing I wasn't accepted into that undergrad art program after all.

Me = Now, once you've reopened your handout, your butterfly should be divided in half. It'll look something like this. (Do the parade wave thing with my handout so students can see what I'm talking about)

Me = OK so, we're gonna be doing a compare and contrast activity with this butterfly, so if you look up here on the dry erase board you'll see the directions.

Jose = This shit is gay.

Deep breath.

I shut my eyelids so the students won't freak out when my eyes actually do roll into the back of my head.

FYI...

Unnecessary cussing, on the part of both high school teachers and high school students, is an occupational hazard at my job.

References to nouns (persons, places, things, or all of the previously mentioned)...

...as being "gay" are also, and unfortunately, common amongst high school male students. Gay, in this regressed state, does not mean **gay**...in the politically correct and quite possibly incorrect sense of the word.

For instance:

Shit synonyms = classwork, assignment, handout.

Gay synonyms = Stupid, lame, pointless...definitely not gay as in, happy or homosexual.

Me = Well...Jose...If this (you're not gonna even try to stop yourself are you?) shit. is. so...gay...you're more than welcome to (don't say it mann...don't say it Neumann, it's totally unneeded) get the hell out of here.

Class is quiet. We all hold our breath in syndicated pause that is collective.

Jose = (Looking up at me as if he didn't actually intend for those words to come out of his mouth) Oh...uhhh...I was just talking about this butterfly Mr. Neumann...it looks like a potato with wings.

Everyone starts laughing.

Internal Me = Ryan, you are a brash idiot.

Me = Ohh...right, yeah, guess it kind of does.

Idiot.

Anthony = Do you have anger management problems Mr. Neumann?

Devin = Yeah Mr. Neumann cuz you know one day you and me is gonna go at it.

Me = Uhhhh...mmm...No? I don't think so. I mean, I'm pretty mellow most of the time...at least I think so. Guess I just can't quite be myself when I'm, ya know, trying to be a teacher person.

Anthony = Yeah, cuz you be buckin on people like it's nothing...

Me = I don't know about all that man...usually it's only if I'm provoked. It's kind of like a switch or a button.

Anthony = Switch?

Me = Yeah, like...I don't know, guess you could say it's like my crazy switch...once it's ON, it's on.

Devin = Oh you mean, like when you threw a student's cell phone against the wall?

Me = What?...(True)...where'd you hear that?

Anthony = Students, Mr. Neumann. We hear stories about you from other students...but me, I just wanna hear some more stories about you and your brother.

Devin = Yeah man, you throw any more sticks at anybody?

Me = Dude...seriously, I mean he spit on me first...twice! actually.

Devin = I know, just kidding...don't go gettin all angry and cussing...

Me = Ha ha, alright jerk, whatever, why don't you get to workin on the assignment. I've got plenty of other stories to tell you 2 some other time.

Anthony = Why don't you just tell us one now? We've still got plenty of time left in class to get this assignment done.

Check my Nokia Go phone for the time...guess they're right. We still have about 45 minutes left in class.

The problem is, I don't know which story to tell them...maybe that one time with the headbtting altercation?...Nahhh...not yet...maayyybeee the throwing incident would be better. Yeah. Throwing.

Me = Alright, here's the deal. Get half the assignment done now, then I'll tell you about a time the crazy switch really went off, but then you need to make sure you use the remaining class time to finish your assignment...OK?

Anthony = Deal.

Devin = Yeah, deal.

Me = Cool.

CONTINUUM

From: Sheree Christopher

To: Ryan Neumann

Subject: Thank you so much

11/10/2009 (12:49PM)

Hey Coach Neumann,

Thanks for the great magazine article you wrote about John and Logan. John showed me the IN THE GAME magazine last night and it was just a delight to read. Before I get choked up again, thanks for all that you do and have meant to John. You are a wonderful influence in his life and we appreciate the time and energy you have put into him.

Sincerely,

Sheree Christopher

John was one of the first students I met at my place of employment. Reflecting on those initial impressions now...almost 4 years later...I don't think there is any way I could have predicted the impact he was going to have on my life as a teacher.

IN THE GAME HIGH SCHOOL SPORTS MAGAZINE
(PLAYER SPOTLIGHT)

2009 Cross Country Runners

by Coach Ryan Neumann

Attend high school with John Christopher for a week...a day even, and you will leave a different person. If one were to act as his shadow, he or she could only hope to mimic the consistently outstanding behavior that is his lifestyle. After coaching John for the past 3 years, I can honestly say that when I think of a positive student role model, he is the first person, perhaps the only person, that comes to mind. John deserves a player spotlight nomination not only because he does the big stuff well (good grades, respectful, open-minded)...but he also does the arguably more important small stuff even better.

For example, John will run a timed 5K on a Thursday afternoon, finish second on the team, walk back down the trail a 1/2 mile to cheer on his teammates who haven't crossed the finish line yet, go home and do his homework that's due on Friday and come in at 7:00 AM that very same Friday to lead an FCA meeting that challenges his peers not only to be good students and good athletes, but all around good people. John demonstrates day in and day out that one must place careful consideration into both his actions and words...

8 semesters ago, John's hormones hadn't quite kicked in so he was still vertically challenged. Fresh out of middle school, the baby of the family, and other than being kind of goofy (which all freshmen are)...that was it.

However, over the past few years, we've gotten to know each other extremely well. In fact, I'd venture to say we know each other so well at this point, that I could no longer be considered his teacher, or even his coach.

Friends.

John's tried to teach me how to dance more times than I care to remember (I refuse to cooperate). We're both fervent music advocates which makes for a constant exchanging of "have you heard this...," or "check this song out." I've driven him home from Cross Country practice over a hundred times. He was at my wedding. I was his Who's Who tapper.

It's kind of strange to mull it all over, and I guess I never really thought about it until Ms. Christopher sent me that email in November. On an inconsequential afternoon prior to that correspondence we were having a conversation and she mentioned something to that same effect...only I remember Ms. Christopher making a reference to the fact that John's dad wasn't really around. He lives up North somewhere, I think. Never really asked John about it, and he's never brought it up...other than expressing a subtle sigh of relief upon finding out a cross country meet conflicted with a previously scheduled trip to see his father. John opted out of the northern exposure and stayed for the race.

Last night I was at Phillips Arena for a John Mayer concert. Went with Mara and some other close friends and I'll have to admit...not a bad way to spend a Wednesday night.

Dude's got some ridiculously insane guitar chops and wasn't afraid to jam out. Before the show we're on the escalator up to our seats, and I'm having this debate in my head.

John's a huge John Mayer fan. Never been to a concert or anything though so I'm thinking...should I get him a souvenir?...would he even want one? ...I mean, it's not like it's a replacement for not being at the concert but hell, it's something right?

Approaching the top of the escalator. Suddenly, an email from earlier this semester flashes through my head; one about separating personal life from professional life. The thought is quickly discarded and we're at the top of the escalator.

Internal Me = Screw it. I'll get him a souvenir.

Mara, Tara, and Ryan walk over to buy some beverages and I stop by the fan stand. T-shirts...CDs...marked up at punch me in the face prices...John Mayer journals...and posters. Do a quick scan and land on this handcrafted poster with all the concert details painted in red, black, and white.

Only 300 made...the sales vender informs and points to the bottom left-hand corner.

122/300.

Sold...save the receipt for next year's tax return? Nahh, not this one.

Roll up the poster. Slide it into this white mailing tube with John Mayer's name and initials tattooed in spiraling red.

Get home from the show (which was awesome!) around midnight and pull the ticket stub out of my pocket.

He'd wanna know what songs were played.

Made a point of memorizing the set list as the show progressed. Before calling it a night I sit down at the kitchen table, jot the 15 song names on the back of the ticket in blue ink and shove it in the mailing tube.

Walk down to the cafeteria during the next day and deliver John's present.

Totally unexpected. Totally ecstatic. Totally worth it.

Like, totally.

BATTLE STUDIES

The decision to charge a student for offenses that are committed while on school property at any time shall be made by the administration of the school.

If the school administration is uncertain as to the interpretation of the CODE OF CONDUCT they are to contact Student Support or their respective Area Assistant Superintendent.

HIGH SCHOOL DISCIPLINE LEVELS

Level 1 Discipline:

Level 1 discipline is used for minor acts of misconduct which interfere with the good order of school.

Following appropriate teacher intervention, students may be referred to an administrator.

Consequences range from administrative conference to three (3) days of In-school Suspension (ISS) and/or restitution.

Example of a Level 1 Offense:

Students who use, display, or turn on communication beepers, cellular phones, video phones, or electronic devices during the regular school day, including instructional class time, class change time, breakfast or lunch...will be charged with a Level 1 Offense.

Likewise, a student may also be charged with a level 1 offense if he/she uses any of the previously mentioned items on school-operated vehicles, including buses.

Level 2 Discipline:

Level 2 discipline offenses are intermediate acts of misconduct.

Students should be referred to an administrator.

Consequences range from Saturday School and/or In-School Suspension (ISS) to five (5) days Out-of-School Suspension (OSS) and/or restitution.

Repeated violations of any Level 2 offense may result in that violation being considered a Level 3 offense which may result in long-term suspension/expulsion.

Example of Level 2 Offense:

1. Students who use any type of profane, vulgar, obscene or ethnically offensive language (written or oral) or gestures...will be charged. **(Level 2-3)**

2. Students who possess or distribute profane, vulgar, pornographic, obscene , or ethnically offensive materials will be also be...uh...reprimanded. **(Level 1-2)**

3. Students who possess ammunition of any kind, including BB's, paint pellets, or CO2 cartridges will be detained as these items are disruptive to the function of the school and may pose a safety risk.

Level 3 Discipline:

Level 3 discipline offenses are serious acts of misconduct including, but not limited to, repeated misbehaviors of a similar nature, serious disruptions of the school environment, threats to health, safety, or property and other serious acts of serious misconduct.

Students must be referred to an administrator. Administrators will notify the appropriate Area Assistant Superintendent, Student Support, and the School District Department of Public Safety (Public Safety), as well as other law enforcement agencies as deemed appropriate. Consequences range from out-of-school-suspension to permanent expulsion and may include referral to apply to the District's Alternative Education Program (AEP). All students accepted into the District's AEP will be on contract, which will include behavior and attendance objectives.

NOTE!

Any misconduct that threatens the health, safety, or well-being of others may result in the immediate suspension of the student from the school and/or school-sponsored activities for up to ten (10) school days, pending disciplinary investigation of the allegations.

NOTED NOTE!

Schools may recommend that a student be considered eligible to apply to attend the AEP during his/her long-term suspension/expulsion. Upon this recommendation or a decision of the District Hearing Panel, expelled long-term suspended students may attend AEP pursuant to a contract.

If the student violates the terms of the contract, he/she may forfeit the opportunity to attend the AEP during the remainder of his/her expulsion or long-term suspension, pursuant to the Order of the Hearing Officer/Panel and/or the terms of the contract.

The student may appeal his/her dismissal from the AEP to the District administrator for the supervision of the AEP. The student may also receive further discipline, in addition to the reinstatement of his/her expulsion or long-term suspension.

Example of Level 3 Offense:

1. Students who participate in any kind of physical altercation.

2. Students who participate in any kind of physical harassment (This can include forms of hazing, intentionally spitting, shanking)

3. Students who display indentified gang tattoos.

4. Students who hold themselves out as members of a gang.

The following reading passage contains discipline infractions from:

A. Level 1-2

B. Level 2-3

C. Levels 1, 2, 3

D. None of the above

Year = 2001.

April.

High School Spring Break (Senior Year)

Panama City, Florida

Holiday Inn (Sunspree) on the Redneck Riviera.

Played (drank) for a whole week...

Time became insignificant. I'd regain consciousness in a hotel room full of empty beer cans, liquor bottles, and cigarette ash.

Natural Light.

Cases upon cases. Average consumption equated to one case per day....so, one beer for every hour of every day for 6 days and 5 nights.

There was however, what one might call, a tipping point.

I was borderline blackout drunk...like on the verge, but not quite...not quite yet. Stagger through the hallway lobby towards the elevators. Wearing sand particles for shoes. Press the arrow indicating upward motion and wait.

Furious.

Fists clenched. Wanna hit something.

Want to hit someone but can't...because it wouldn't be right...right?...right...would only make things worse.

[Ding]

Elevator lands.

Enter.

Stumble.

Punch 4.

Doors close.

Inside of the elevator is that low-grade reflective metal stuff. You can kinda see yourself but you kinda can't. See the shape of a person.

Envision the outline of your former self.

Want so badly to punch someone but can't...what can I hit what can I hit what can I destroy what I can break...inanimate objects?

Land on 4 but the doors haven't opened yet.

Angst consumes.

See the amorphous shape that is myself. Pierce the unpolished metal and begin to beat the hell out of my reflective disposition. Jam floor buttons 5 through 10 so they're permanently lit up. Punch the button causing doors to remain open and lose it...strike the interior elevator walls until all the knuckles on my right hand are cracked and broken.

Heart racing. Step off the elevator. Glasses fog up.

Blind.

March, 2010

(my place of employment)

Moo's feet are securely fastened to the worn down wax outside Room 300. Back against a row of blue lockers. Some wear gentle dents. Others use fluorescent glares to disguise idiosyncratic scuff marks.

Temperamental adolescents...and/or adolescence, may impair one's ability to operate heavy machinery.

Staring in one direction (straight). Swaying from side to side as if he were on a boat...Moo's feet haven't budged.

Conscious. Eyes open...buutttt...no one's there. Furrowed brow.

Clenched fists. Bloody knuckles.

Bloody knuckles remind me of Panama City.

Right hand...index and middle knuckles = bright red liquid...like ink from a teacher's grading pen. Just a flesh wound.

Close the door to Room 3oo so it's just me and Moo in the hallway. I would say the silence is absolute, but when no one speaks, the building breathes with impeccable clarity.

Me = ...hheeyyyy mannn (hesitant to say anything at all)....youuuu ok?

Moo (nickname) slants his head to the left.

Moo = ...got kicked out of class. (looks distraught)

Me = ...alright. Ummmm...well, I don't want to pry or anything, buutt, is there anything I can do?...or uh, do you need anything?

Moo redirects his gaze forward once more. Thinking.

Moo = ...what?...you wanna know why I got kicked out?

Me = Well...I mean, yeah, but ya know, only if you feel comfortable telling me...I mean, it's really none of my business.

In the 4 years I've spent as a certified teacher, I've taught one 12th grade literature class. Last fall, Contemporary Literature was my one and only block with true 12th graders. Moo was in that class and I discovered that he's got...aaaa uh temper...for lack of a better word. At that point in time, he was a senior behind on credits...
in desperate need of that credit light at the end of the tunnel.

Cue Neumann.

Moo = Sometimes I feel like a bitch Mr. Neumann.

Me = What!?...what are you talking about man?

Moo = I mean...these kids. Today. Like this kid, challenging my presentation...tryin to call me out in front of class because he think he know more than I do when really...really, we both probably know the same amount of information and he don wanna show me any respect...I try to ignore it. Went back to my seat. Sat down and he's still talking ya know...sayin whadda you know about this and that...and I'm like, you know, I'm tryin not to say anything and then he says, can you believe this, he says, "Whad the fuck you sayin anyway." An after that Mr. Neumann...after thay, I just lost it.

Me = Hmmm...well what do you mean, lost it?

Moo = Well (insert shoulder shrug) You know, I cussed em out. Told em I was gonna kill em an...

Me = ..Whoa!..wait!...what?...

Moo = I told em I could kill em. Mr. Neumann, I ain't afraid of fightin...I jus would rather avoid the consequences.

Me = So you weren't serious?

Moo = ...Nah, I mean, don't get me wrong Mr. Neumann, I only need one punch and that's it, but once I fight, ain no stoppin me. I mean, only thing that kept me from, well, one of the only things that kept me from fightin in class was my teacher...I didn't wanna take the chance of accidentally hittin her...cause if I hit her...well, I'm done.
Me = True. But ya know, sayin stuff like that can get you in trouble too.

Moo = Why?

Me = Cause man, stuff like that makes people...I don't know, not panic, but, they're gonna be like, whoa! what's this guy talkin about?

Moo's contemplating. Times like this, I'm ever so thankful to have a co-teacher. Mr. J's been covering class since I stepped in the hall with Moo. Left class at 9:33AM and it's almost 10:00AM now.

Me and Moo have been walking around the school and conversating. Well, he's been talking and I've been trying to listen. Come to find out, Moo wasn't waiting in the 300 hallway to talk to me...he was waiting in the hallway to jump the kid he was having problems with...was gonna take him in the bathroom and let out some pent up hostility. Here's the catch though, Moo failed one of his graduation tests last year. If he gets suspended for fighting, there's a good possibility that he won't be able to retake the exam he failed...which means he won't graduate which means, badness.

Hello intervention.

Moo = You know why I like talking to you Mr. Neumann?

Me =...nope.

Moo = Cause you a good listener.

Me = Ohh, well thanks man.

Moo = Well you are, but look...this whole thing, it don even matter about this kid right. Like, I'm just angry. Mr. Neumann...you ever been so mad you forgot where the anger even came from?

Me = Ha ha...uhh, yeah man, definitely.

2001.

Panama City, Florida.

Concrete Stucco. Outward appearance of the Holiday Inn resembled Concrete Stucco.

Drunk, numb, angry, and alone.

Walking the perimeter of whatever floor I'm on. See at this hotel, it's open, so...every room door meets the outside...no internal hallways...the building bends into a weak U. Doors are on the outside of the U and balconies are on the inside.

Knuckles are pre-cut and I can't feel anything.

Decide it would be a good idea to drag my hand along the concrete stucco walkway until I feel something. Don't know how long I was actually walking...but by the time I can feel...blood drips awkwardly down my fingers and I can tell it's gonna be one of those scarring ordeals.

March, 2010

Moo = Well, if you been so angry you didn know what to do...what happened?

Me =What do yo mean?

Moo = Like, how did you get rid of the anger.

Me = I don't know if ever did man. I mean, I'm sure I did but I don't know when. I started running...I did a lot of writing...and I gave myself some scars.

Moo = Scars?

Me = yeah, you can't really see them anymore...they've faded...but when it gets cold out, my knuckles turn like, purple and blue and black...exactly where I busted my knuckles senior year in high school...that's when I remember...that's when I kind of...relive the whole thing.

But look, what I learned, it's not worth it. Now maybe that's a lesson you need to learn on your own but I'm just telling ya...it might be easier to talk it out.

Moo = I know I know...

Me = Anyway, look man...we've got like, what, 5 minutes until the bell rings. What do you want to do?

Moo =I ain't gonna do anything Mr. Neumann. Walking around the school helped me cool down. Thanks. But look, I ain't gonna cause any trouble. I'm not as mad anymore. We can go back to my class.

Me = But what if that kid says something...again?

Moo = (insert shoulder shrug) Well, I can't control him. I can only control me.

Me = Well said.

Moo = Look, I'll be fine Mr. Neumann.

We come to an agreement. Moo doesn't go back to class. Bell rings. Classes change. Later that day, I see Moo and his offender walking down a different hallway, sorting things out peaceably.

WIMPY KID

"I got the 4th book!"

Sent: SUNDAY (March 14, 2010)

3:42:35 PM

"Did you get my text?"

The door to Room 300 is open. Lights ON. Hallway quiet. Was taking in the last few minutes of silence when Laran caught me off guard with the whole early morning talking thing.

MONDAY (March 14, 2010)

7:53:00AM

Me = ...whoa there!...what was that?

Laran = Did you get my text?

Me = ...text?...ohhhh yeaaahhh (thinking, thinking, what did it say?)...you got the 4th book. How do you like it?

Laran = Don't know yet...still reading the 3rd.

Laran was in my American Literature class last semester. About midway through the semester, he developed a voracious appetite for graphic novels...freaking devours the things.

Backpack resting on a dirty desktop, Laran unzips the bag,

shuffles through some binders, and pulls out the 4th book.

Bright Yellow. **Diary of a Wimpy Kid (Dog Days)...Jeff Kinney.**

They (I have no idea who) are making a movie out of the first book. Comes out sometime soon I think. April maybe.
Laran= Here you go. (He hands me the book)

Me = Well wait, you haven't even read it yet. Don't you want to read it first?

Laran = I gotta finish the 3rd remember? Just bring it back on Monday.

Me = Monday?...

Laran = ...or whenever you finish reading it.

Me = You sure?

Laran = Yeah, just don't forget this time.

Laran let me borrow the 3rd book a couple weeks ago. Gave it to me on a Monday, then I was out for 3 days, totally forgot I even had the book, and by the time I returned, I'd completely forgotten it was somewhere in my possession. Took me until the following Tuesday to remember...

...can't let that happen again.

Me = No worries! But hey...can you send me a text later on in the week to remind me?

Laran = Sure. I gotta go. See ya Neumann.

Me = See ya man.

As Laran is walking out a teacher from a couple doors down walks in.

"Neu!"

Me = (Holding the brightly binded book in my hands) Yes ma'am. Morning.

Ms. Kamila = Morning. I need a battery for my...what are yoouuu reading?

Me = Oh, uh, Diary of Wimpy Kid, heard of it?

Ms. Kamila = Uhh, ha, yeah. My daughter is reading that.

Me = Oh, cool!

Ms. Kamila = She's in 2nd grade Neums.

Ms. Kamila laughs a little. John, Richard, and Palmer entered the class while Ms. Kamila and I were talking...they're laughing too.

Me = Oh...

Ms. Kamila = Something you're not telling us Neums?

Me = (insert shoulder shrug) uhhh...I'm a 2nd grader trapped in a 27 year old body?

Laran = Sure. I gotta go. See ya Neumann.

John and Richard listen to our conversation intently. Palmer walks silently over to the dry erase board to inspect his drawing. It's been up for the past few weeks and he usually strolls in for touch-up work in the mornings. He also adds his thought of the day.

The right-hand side of the dry erase board is reserved for Palmer because...well, I never use it and he seems to get a kick out of decorating Room 300 with his artwork...this from the student who refused to do any actual work, or even come to school, during the first 6 weeks of school last spring...when he was a student of mine.

His latest drawing is pretty good too...a charicature of Rambo.

Palmer is in charge of Rambo's thought bubble on a weekly basis. More often than not, the "thought of the day" is umm...random to say the least. So far, it's blank today. Palmer is thinking.

By the time Ms. Kamila and I finish talking it's 8:19AM.

Hall duty becons...must. stand. by. classroom. door.

John and Richard stand beside the door with me and debate the very likely possibility that I was, in fact, a wimpy kid.

Me = I don't know if I was wimpy...I mean, I was definitely nerdy but wimpy...I don't know man...

Richard = Sure, coach.

Me = Whatever dude.

John and Richard both laugh and say their parting farewells. Palmer strolls, as per usual, out of Room 300 with the standard:

"See ya later Lund."

Me = Later jerk.

Palmer = Ha ha ha...don't forget to read the board.

1st block students enter Room 300, bell rings, door closes, eyes look to Rambo.

Rambo thinks...

Neumann was the wimpy kid in his days.

NEUMANIA

the-oc-ra-cy

[thee-**ok**-ruh-see]

-noun.

A form of government in which God or a deity is recognized as the supreme civil ruler, the God's or deity's laws being interpreted by the ecclesiastical authorities.

Word Origin & History

1622, "sacerdotal government under divine inspiration" (as that of Israel before the rise of kings), from Gk. theokratia "the rule of God" (Josephus), from theos "god" + kratos "a rule, regime, strength".

Thank you dictionary.com.

"Get a new car?"

Me = Oh...uhhh...nope. Why?...you like?

Palmer is referring to the navy blue minivan behind me.

Palmer = (shoulder shrug + look of indifference) Mmmm...thought you drove that blue station-wagon thing.

Me = I do. Cracked windshield. Gettin fixed. My parents let me borrow their minivan for a few days. Pretty sweet huh? I used to drive it in high school.

Palmer = Ha ha.

County issued computer bag slung across my right shoulder. Pot of coffee, travel mug, and some unorganized papers share space in the reusable lime green Publix bag I'm holding in my right hand. Sliding door on the right side of my mom's Chevy Venture remains open.

Me = Check this out.

Press the automatic sliding door icon on the key chain. Door closes by itself. Hands-free...well, almost...hands-free technology circa 1996.

Me = Pretty cool eh?

Palmer looks at me with a blank stare, then at the van, then at me.

Palmer= eh...no. Not at all Neumann.

Me = Whatever....Walking in?

Palmer = Yeah.

The student parking lot is a fragmented sheet of fading asphalt. Every morning, pieces of gravel and bits of shattered glass echo in automotive wheel wells as I migrate to my predetermined parking space.

Drowsy...sparsely populated with vehicular contraptions...Palmer and I walk through the lot towards the main entrance of school. More and more cars are beginning to enter the school zone but it's still somewhat early. Sparrows flutter from the undercarriage of portable trailers (classrooms) to a woven metal fence. Perched in the open spaces as if in a tree, they chirp and sputter away when our encroachment becomes to invasive.

Me = Sooo uh, did you have like aaaa...create a country project?...or something like that recently?

Palmer = (laughing to himself) Why do you ask?

Me = Well, Montoya was up in the English office for something last week and she said there were these two guys in her class that used me in their project or something...

Palmer = Ha ha. Sooo, how'd you know it was me?

Me = I didn't at first. But Montoya was telling me about the projects you all had to do...like, creating a country, and that you guys named your country Neumania and that the flag for the country was my school picture for this year.

Palmer = Ha ha ha ha ha ha ha!

At the beginning of every school year, just like students, teachers are asked to pose for yearbook pictures. Necessary evil I guess; depending on the level of enjoyment one gets while employing fake smiles. Me = none.

So then, a few weeks later, after the superficial happiness has all but been forgotten, a bazillion self portraits appear in each participatory teacher's mailbox. 5 X 7's, 4 X 6's, wallet size, and then if you're really lucky, you get one of those 8.5 X 11's that are the perfect size for dart boards.

Typically, I extract my pictures from one drawer and shove them into another, less used drawer where they may remain buried beneath paperwork I choose to neglect.

Palmer likes to investigate the drawers in Room 300. Earlier this year he found my yearbook pictures and decided to hold on to them, like...all of them, without me realizing it.

Me = Yeah yea yea. So, what was it? What was the project?

Palmer = What you said pretty much. We were all assigned a different type of government, and ummm, using that government, we had to like, create a country. I did the drawings and Lyle did the writing.

Me= Oh, cool. What kind of government did you get?

Palmer = Theocracy...which is like, a government where the ruler is chosen by god or something. We chose you.

Me = Ha ha ha...are you serious?...that's ridiculous.

Palmer = Ha ha, yeah...we used your picture as the flag and named our country **Neumania**.

Me = Ha ha...jerk!...can't believe you stole my yearbook pictures.

Palmer = Shouldn't have made them so easy to get to...I still have like, 8 of those wallet size ones.

Me = Dude!...they were buried in a...ahhhh, whatever. Ha ha, keep 'em...didn't wantem anyways.

We enter the school lobby and walk under painted blue lettering that says, PROUD TO BE AN EAGLE. Paths diverge and the school day proceeds.

Flash forward to the end of the day and I'm in Room 300 gathering my stuff before heading out the door. Lyle walks in with a devious smirk on his face.

Lyle = Hey, Mr. Neumann.

Me = Oh hey man! What's going on? Haven't see you in awhile.

Lyle = Yeah. Oh, nothing. I'm good. Found this in the bathroom...is this yours?

Lyle hands me a wallet-size piece of paper.

Lyle = Yeah it was really weird, like, it was tapped above one of the sinks in the boys bathroom and it said, Neumann is God.

WTF.

I flip over the wallet-size piece of paper to see an artificial smile gleaming back at me. My yearbook picture. Only, it appears that Palmer's done a little redecorating. An eye patch, goatee, and missing teeth have been added in black sharpie.

Me = I look like a pirate.

Lyle = Ha ha ha ha ha ha ha.

Me = (Trying not to laugh, but…can't because well, it is kinda funny) ha ha ha ha ha ha.

Theocracy. Scary thought.

NIGHT SCHOOL

1 New Text Message

[Sunday Night]

Menu.

Messages.

Inbox.

(Closed Envelope) **Andre.**

(Open Envelope) **Andre Text = Neumannator are we still on for the night school rides next week cause its 3 more people besides me are in need of a ride also but i call shotgun in advance alright**

Me Text = Yep. We're still on. Who are the other 3 people? Oh and where is night school? what time does it start? and what time do we need to leave school?

Andre Text = The twins and a girl named naseme (nay + seem) and its on dallas hwy and we need to leave around four or like four fifteen somewhere around there and my mother will pick us up from there i'll try to get you some gas money alright thanks

Me Text = No worries about the gas money. I'd rather you guys graduate on time. See you tomorrow.

Andre Text = Thanks neumannator

Me Text = No prob!

Andre Text = We'll all come up to your room after school now out of monday thru thursday how many days could you help me with

Me Text = Monday through thursday

Andre Text = Thank you man thank you very much neumann

Me Text = No worries man. yous is welcome.

Andre Text = Yous is not a word by the way

Me Text = I know, just making sure you were paying attention jerk :)

Andre Text = Ha ha no yous just cant spell

Me Text = Whatever dude

Andre Text = Yes i WIN

Night School is, more or less, a last chance for seniors who are behind on credits but still want to graduate from high school in 4 years.

Basically, night school is a credit recovery situation where students attend an additional 3 hours of school (5PM-8PM) at an alternative education locale somewhere in the county.

Students attend night school for about 6 weeks, Monday-Thursday, in an attempt to recovery previous shortcomings.

Andre is one of those students.

Last week, his car broke down...again.

He reaaallllyyy needs to graduate...like, really.

He needs to get out of high school and away from all the potentially hazardous situations he tends to get himself into.

There are many other students like Andre at my school. Guess the problem I have with Andre though, is that I know him better than all those other students...which makes it difficult when I hear about, and, on occasion, see some of the stupid shit he does.

But I'm not his father.

Right now, his father is wandering the streets of Atlanta.

Several missions are within walking distance of where Mara and I live. Known Andre for about 2 years at this point, which means I've known his father is homeless for about the same amount of time.

I walk and run around the city pretty frequently. Every time I talk to a homeless man, or...every time a homeless man talks at me, I wonder if I'm talking to Andre's dad...I wonder...if we came to that realization...if we discovered that we were both connected through Andre...

I wonder if we'd have anything to talk about?

Ryan Lund Neumann

EXORCISE

True story. I had a babysitter the first nine years of my life. Her name was Mary Brant, but we called her Gunga. She dies of lung cancer midway through my freshman year of college, so about a week later I sit down and write a letter to Gunga's husband. I tell him everything she would have wanted to hear, what the campus looks like, what my grades are, how much I miss their company and all that. A real sentimental piece. Then I tell a few stories to make my point, how I make breadcrumbs and eggs for dinner at least once a week the way Gunga used too, how my roommate thinks that particular combination of ingredients is weird as shit (although I don't write "shit"), especially considering I eat it with ketchup. I tell him the weather up here in the mountains is a little crazy, for sure, but crazy in a good way, because it's challenging, and each day I'm beginning to realize I like testing myself, just man against nature. Appalachian State is a great, great place, I say.

Anyway, it's an awesome letter, very poignant and heartfelt. I almost weep writing it. Get all choked up about the good times my brother, sister, and I had with Gunga, how she taught us to shuffle a deck of cards, teaching us about Noah's Arc through a Nintendo game while she sat on the couch chain smoking cigarettes. A very compassionate human being. Like the time a storm knocked two baby cardinals out of a tree and the next morning Gunga found them. Probably the coolest pets in domesticated history. She named the pair Punch and Judy.

171

They used to untie my shoes while I sat there eating Kix for breakfast. Don't see shit like that outside a Disney movie, I say. His wife, she had the right idea. She knew how to teach. Few months before her death, on this real overcast and dull morning, I walk across campus to the post office and find a letter from Gunga in my P.O. box. Written in old school cursive, the way cursive is supposed to look, I describe his wife's letter the way I remember it, and tell him that I carry her words with me in my wallet.

And then the letter gets very solemn. Try asking him a few nonspecific questions so as to sound generic, but at some point I just let go. How are you? How was the funeral? What was Gunga like during her last few days? I apologize for not being there and try to explain why I was not there; even though I, myself, find the explanation inexcusable. I don't tell him how helpless I felt the last time I spoke to Gunga on the phone. I don't mention that I was sitting on a curb in single-digit weather while snow fell to the ground the last time I heard her voice. I sure as hell don't admit that I was about to cry when I realized the Gunga I was speaking to on the phone that night, the one who had not fully recovered from a stroke, was not the same Gunga I once knew. I've never told anyone when she said, "Love you, Ryan," one last time, it was the first time I had ever said, "Love you, too" and meant every damn word of it. Conclude the letter by saying I'll call soon and hope that he's doing well until then.

So what happens? Letter goes in the mail.

To this day, the jerk's never written back.

A true teacher story is not moral. It does not instruct, nor promote ethical thought, nor lay the foundation for appropriate human behavior, nor restrain people from doing the things people have always done. If a story seems to have a moral, second guess it. If at the end of a teacher's story you feel uplifted, or if you feel that some small fragment of righteousness has been restored to your disillusioned identity, then you have been made the victim of a very old and horrible lie. There is no righteousness. Ethics do not exist. Therefore, as a general rule, you can tell a true teacher story by its absolute and uncompromising adherence to the obscenely absurd. Pay attention to the word choice. Jerk, I say. I do not say asshole. I certainly do not say bastard. Then I avert my eyes and stare. I'm 27 years old. To this day, it's still too much for me--so I look at my computer screen with these big sad overcast eyes and say jerk, because this motherly figure that helped raise me is dead, and because it's so inescapably sad and true: he never wrote back.

You can tell a true teacher story if it embarrasses you. If you don't care for vulgarity, you don't care for the truth; if you don't care for the truth, watch what you read. Send people to teach, they come home bitching and moaning.

Listen: "I mean, I write this really emotional letter, I slave over it, and what happens? To this day, the jerk's never written back."

I usually tell this story before unveiling my students' final exam. Questions interrupt before we ever get into specifics.

So...what's the point? Like, why'd you even take the time to write the letter if he didn't write back? Have you spoken to him since? How long ago was this?

Sometimes you just need to write. Doesn't matter if the intended audience reads what you wrote or not. It's like, well...it's like, exorcising demons, I say. I laugh when I say it. Not sinister or anything, but comical. Not everyone can communicate what they feel, whether it be words, actions, or a combination of the two. Sometimes you just need to...to, say.

HACK ATTACK

One Sunday afternoon towards the end of middle school, while we were all pretending we knew, for sure, who we were, I found myself on the losing end of a fistfight. It was about something stupid–one false clique (skaters) versus another false clique (preps)–but even so the "fight" was humiliating. There was no back and forth. Adam Hacker (prep) was, and still is, much bigger and much stronger than me (skater), and before I even knew which way was up Hacker had me pinned down and proceeded to punch me square in the face.

Imagine several of your closest friends, and several of your not so closest friends, gathered round you in a circle, heads hovering in ecstatic awe over what they're seeing. Hacker hit me hard. And he didn't stop at first. They said my face made this hollow thud sound, like a hammer on a piece of drywall, but even then Hacker did not hesitate, and back then, before we discovered booze, Hacker had the kind of punch that did not miss. No one had to pull him off. For some reason, he just stopped. When it was over, our buddy's dad picked us up and I sat in the far back of their red Jeep Cherokee, where I could still feel the adrenaline rushing through my veins, and where 10 minutes later, when we got back to the neighborhood, no one spoke of what had happened.

In many other stages of life it might've ended there. But this was middle school, where nothing was off limits, and where hormones were so jacked up you couldn't even tell right from wrong if you wanted to, so I started to worry. After all, still had school on Monday. It was mostly in my head. But it never occurred to me, maybe not until now, that I was not, and never have been, mad about the whole thing. Might have had a little resentment, but never any malicious intent. That Monday after there were no threats of retaliation from me, no vows of revenge (mainly because I wouldn't have been able to even if I tried), just a silent tension between Hacker and myself that lasted until our senior year of high school.

"Have you ever been in a fight?...Missterr uhhhh, teacher guy."

Cautiously, almost reluctantly, I will admit, "yes."

"Did you win?"

That's always the next question.

Me = Ehhhhhh, well, depends on which fight we're talking about.

"You been in more than one!?!?"

Me = ...uhhhmmmm, yeeeaahh.

"How many fights have you been in, Misstterrrr uhhhhh, mister, teacher, Neu guy?"

Me = It's...kind of hard to say.

They never ask where. Like, "Where did you learn how to fight?" Or, "How did you learn to fight?"

Now that, in my opinion, is the fucking question...How did you learn?

And I must say, for some strange reason, it all comes back to the Hack Attack.

Sometimes instead of "teaching," I tell stories.

Some days, when I've covered every possible component of my lesson plan, and there's still 15 minutes left of class time, I'll do anything to keep them quiet and in their seats.

They think I'm teaching.

Hell, even I think I'm teaching.

To be honest, I am learning.

Over the past 5 years, I can honestly say that I have learned something new, every...single...day. There are days when I am wwaaayyyyy more than a teacher. There are days when I barely teach. In Room 300 I am a police officer, a father figure, someone to confide in, an authoritarian, a comedian, a wannabe professor, a bookkeeper, a bystander, an idiot, a guidance counselor, a cog, a facilitator, an apologist, a hippie, a team leader, a coach, a politician, an employee, a hallway monitor, a couples therapist, a jerk, a brother, a big kid, a check-in-the-box, a vault, a cynic, a student, the last line of defense.

I've had other teachers advise me, "Ryan, they shouldn't be calling you Neumann. They should call you Mr. Neumann. They don't need to know everything about you. They don't need to know anything about you. They are children. You are the adult. You are the one in charge of your classroom. You are in control. You know that, right? They're not the ones running shit around here, you are. Give them an inch and they'll take a mile. You are not their friend. Did you hear me? You are not...their...friend."

But ya see, the thing is, about that whole control thing...it's the other way around. Take this past winter for example. Snowpacalypse 2011 happens. Freezing rain makes the transportation of students to school impossible because this is Georgia. No students, no school. No students, no teach. No teach, no teacher. What students don't realize is that they really are the ones in control. They are, in a sense, the ones running shit around here. If they don't come to class, my job, for all intensive, salary-based purposes, becomes nonexistent.

It's a tricky game. When they raise their hands and put on these genuine looks of interest and ask me what I was like in high school or why I wear those black Converse or who those people are in the picture frames I have stuck to my dry erase board or why my dry erase board is covered with pictures and stuff instead of writing and stuff...tricky tricky. They know teachers. They've heard about bell-to-bell instruction and what no part of it, so they'll ask questions to redirect...and many times, misdirect the lesson.

What I'm learning though, is that I don't mind telling these stories about my former years as long as I can tie them into class. Ya know, so that, just when everyone thinks they've escaped having to write about this or that, I can ask them to think and write about something basic...and then that one basic question will lead us into transcendentalism or Faulkner or whatever, A Letter from Birmingham Jail.

I tell them about that Monday in middle school. How, for the most part, everything was going pretty well. Didn't have anyone pointing and laughing at me in the hallway. No whisperers on the other side of the classroom laughing when they found out I didn't even get a swing in.

And then I got to P.E. Must have been our basketball unit or something because we were playing "Gotcha!" So we're going through the rotation, standing on the free throw line, one person shoots and if they make it they're good. Retrieve the ball and pass it to the next person in line. If you miss, you've gotta hurry up, grab your ball, and make a layup before the guy directly behind you shoots his free throw...and if he makes his before you make yours, you're shit out of luck.

So were playing gotcha and the kid behind me is giving me this weird look all class. Like he knows something I don't. Finally I ask him, "Eh Jason...uhh...you OK."

He starts laughing.

Jason = Yeah. (insert hahahaha) Heard you got the shit (although I should probably say shhhhtttufff because this is school, right? And I only cuss when I'm irritated, right?) beat out of you by Hacker.

Then I pause.

Me and Adam Hacker did not become instant buddies, but we did learn to tolerate one another.

Wait..."Me and Adam Hacker?" Aren't you an English teacher? What's your definition of proper English?

I don't know...rhythm maybe. Anyway, me and Adam Hacker did not become instant buddies, but we did learn to tolerate one another. Over the next few years his presence became a regular thing in the neighborhood.

He became fast friends with some fellas who shared an enthusiasm for seeing just how much a person could get away with. They'd cover each other on garage hopping patrol, share cigarettes, and take turns playing wing-man for one another. In late April of our senior year he apologized to me while we were taking a piss at the Holiday Inn in Panama City. As far as I could tell he was serious. We'd already been drinking for hours, and I had no desire to relive unflattering moments from my awkward middle school development, but out of nowhere, he just started talking. And then in July of that same year I kneed him in the balls. It was an accident. He'd just parked his Blazer in the cul-de-sac, got out, then he grabbed me in this big ole bear hug and lifted me off the ground. "Neumann!" he said.

Internal Me = Oh, damn.

For what seemed like a while I kept thinking, "Damn it, how the hell am I gonna get out of this?"

Then I kind of panicked.

Tried to get out of the tree trunks that were his arms, but there wasn't much I could do. Tried to push off with my elbows. When that didn't work I thought I'd try using my legs since they were just dangling there off the ground. And that's when I kneed him in the balls. Total accident.

He fell hard.

I finally had some breathing room.

"Damn Neumann!"

Me = ...euhhh, shit man, I'm uhh...sorry.

Hack Attack = What the hell Neumann, just foolin around, didn't have to knee me in the nuts. Fuck!

10 years later, he hasn't forgotten.

"Neumann," he'll say. "Don't knee me in the balls."

If I could revisit my 23rd year, my first year as a teacher, I'd take me out for a burger, some sweet potato tots, and several obscure, if otherwise unknown, high gravity beers. I'd have a real sincere, all bullshit aside, conversation with myself. The type of discussion I'd remember for the rest of my life. Dialogue so deep I'd be dwelling on the words years later, waiting for the day it would be okay to write about such things.

I'd say look, Ryan, fucking relax, man. Stand up straight. Stop drinking those damn energy drinks, and speak up. Stop saying "yes" to everyone who asks you to do them a favor. Stop apologizing for shit you're not even remotely sorry for, and stop putting yourself down. You wouldn't punch yourself in a fistfight would you? Hell no, so why do it when you speak?

I'd listen to myself. I'd soak up the sum.

You, of all people, are starting your teaching career. You, who once feared public speaking more than death, will instruct generations far beyond that of your indifference. This is not going to be easy, I'd say. I know. I've been doing it for 5 years now. Thought about giving up more times than I can count. You'd be better off as a UFC fighter actually.

At least there'd be people paying you get the shit kicked out of you. As a teacher, the greatest asset you have at your disposal is the life you have lived. If you don't learn to use it, well shit man, I don't know what to tell you.

Somebody should have told me, Hey, Neumann, your "career", Mr.
Neumann, the next 5 years of it, man, is gonna be AYP (adequate yearly
progress), AYP, AYP, students, students, students, standards,
standards, standards, rubrics and essential questions, rubrics and
essential questions, boxes of assignments piling up in your filing
cabinet (<–trashcan), in your car, at home, days, nights catching up on
emails, school improvement committees, cross country practice,
failure reports, meetings...all fucking kinds of meetings,
recommendation letters, and don't forget about lesson plans, and
grading, oh yeah, grading...grading the work of hundreds, maybe even
thousands if you stay in this game long enough, can you imagine that?
I mean shit, you're not even teaching yet. I've been doing this for 5
years and it's still hard for me to fathom. Thousands of misplaced
teenagers, a few hundred technologically savvy men and women. You
won't even want to read Best Sellers by the time you get done. Forget
Oprah's booklist. Forget all of that, man. You won't even want to read.
Period. You'll go def, dumb, and blind doing what your about to be
doing. An interstate of adolescent shtuff, Neumann...straight to the
sea. Where oceans bleed into the sky. You won't know up from down.

They'll do a lobotomy on you one day because of the all crazy shit
that's stuck in your head. Hundreds upon thousands of teenage
hardships and nonexistent home lives. They'll cut those nerves, man.
Intractable mental disorder. That's you. Smile for the camera.

You'll get done with your second year of teaching, and Neumann, let
me tell ya, it will be one hell of a year, and you're going to ask yourself:

"Is this it?" It'll sound like a Strokes album but it's so much bigger than
that. "Is this it...is this my life? Am I gonna stick this out? Can I do this
for 30+ years?"

Remember dude, this is their world, you just live in it. So, that makes
you one of them, a teenager for life. Fountain of Youth, eternal
sunshine of the spotless mind...you got it buddy. Welcome. You're
living on two different planets. Monday through Friday, August to
May, and you'll never be fully aware. Ryan, you'll never really be sure
what this profession is doing to you...what type of person you're
becoming...what they're molding you into. This is high school

remember? Probably the most insecure time to be alive but the thing is, they're only in it for 4 years, you're in this for life, man...life.

Summer will come and it'll be see ya later, Mr. Neumann, my brother, although he's really not my brother we just use it as a term of endearment, my brother's gonna request you for the fall, and don't go flipping anymore tables OK, but uh yeah, I'll see you in August. HAGS.

But there's something more. You know that, Ryan, don't you? In your classroom, in Room 300, something is always happening. It'll never be dull, for sure. Despite your desire for routine, there will be no routine. No monotony. Your students, they'll keep you sharp. You'll never grow old, but the things is, you may have the mind of a 17 year old male forever. That's what might get you in trouble, Neumann. You'll get used to meeting your students on their level.

Talking to them as such...as equals. And you won't mind telling them stories about your youth, your real youth, and won't think twice about mentioning this guy you grew up with, a guy who, to this day greets you with,"Neumann, don't knee me in the balls."

I tell my students there's going to be things you remember. Words that stick with you. Things that people say to you, or about you, that you just can't shake. Crystallized fragments of vocabulary. Frozen in ice.

"Heard you got the shit beat out of you by Hacker."

Then I pause.

They want to know what happened next but I won't give them that inch. I want the mile first.

Me = I don't know.

Students = What do you mean you don't know?

Me = What would you have done?

Then they realize, dammit, he's done it again. We're gonna have to write about this, they'll think. He really wants to know what we would have done...how would we have, responded...or whatever. And they'll be right.

Me = I want to know what you would have done? How you would have responded...or whatever.

Allow me to be frank. I am now twenty eight years old, and would love nothing more than to be able to write, for a living, and about 15 years ago when I was in P.E. some kid, well not just some kid, Jason Sassen, like I'd forget his name, said, "Heard you got the shit beat out of you by Hacker," while we were playing Gotcha. Almost everything I tell my classes after this choice phrase I invent.

I wouldn't say it's so much a lie, though. It's a search for authenticity.

Like right here, now, as I relive the past, I'm thinking about everything I would have felt at that point in time...everything I would have wanted to do...to say. For instance, I'd like to tell you I did this: 15 years ago I was baited while playing Gotcha in P.E.

My eyes grew wide, and my mouth drew tight, like George freaking Mcfly right before he lays a haymaker on Biff at the end of Back to the Future. I stopped bouncing my basketball, strangled it with two hands, and chucked at point blank range into the nose of Jason Sassen. You could hear cartilage pop. You could see how off center his nose was after the deflection. Made your head turn sideways. You could feel the blood pouring from his nose like a faucet onto the shiny waxed floor. I could see my fluid reflection in the dark red puddle. But ya see, that never happened. I want my students to feel how I felt. I want to tell them that writing, good writing, makes you feel...and that much of the time, storytelling truth is waaaayyyyy more true than what had actually happened.

Here's what actually happened.

I was in middle school and Jason Sassen said, ""Heard you got the shit beat out of you by Hacker."

I thought we were cool, ya know. Not friends necessarily, but not enemies either. Understood acquaintances. But when he said that, I knew we weren't. I didn't know what to say. Could feel the anger building up inside but didn't know what to do. Fighting wasn't an option. I wasn't that kind of kid. Couldn't risk getting suspended, what would Mom and Dad think?

I didn't do anything. Just took it; took the jab and bottled up the anger.

Here's the storytelling truth.

Jason was a lanky, brown haired, skater in my P.E. class. He fell to the center of the court after I pegged him with the basketball. When Mr. Weiss hustled over to help Jason up off the floor, he left a trail of red shoe prints leading to the exit door. I stood there motionless. Ghostly white. Unbelieving of what I had just done, but unable to erase an increasingly shameless thought, "Who beat the shit out of who, now, asshole." I hurt him.

What good writing can do, and I'm by no means an expert, but what I'm slowly finding out is that good storytelling can make all of this real.

I just likes to write, I tell them. I want you guys to likes writing too...but we need to practice, we need to write. So now, when I do write, I'm beginning to realize there are no limitations. There are no boundaries. I can attach the people from my life to these abstract ideals and...ideas.

I can talk without interruption. I can tell you everything. I can tell you nothing.

"Missstterrr uh, Watkins, errr I mean Mellman, ohhppp, I mean, what's your name, teacher guy, Neu guy, Neumann," so like, how are we going to know when you're telling the truth?...because, like, you basically told us that you make stuff up so that we can, like, feel how you felt orrr..."

Me = (shrug of the shoulders) I don't know.

Student = What?

Me = If nothing else, I guess, as long as you're questioning that sort of idea, like what is true and what is not true, I don't think it really matters...at least not right now, not with the way I'm asking you to think about writing.

Student(s) = I don't get it...yeah...me neither....huhhhh?

As a teacher, you get used to talking in circles too.

But then sometimes, like on Friday nights, when I go to the bar and am hanging out with friends I forget how to communicate. The words escape me. So, my friends will look at me like, eh Neumann, pretty quiet down there. You OK? Come on Gramps, they'll say. Lock it up. They'll look at me and I won't be sure what to say...or what the most clever response is, because this spaced-out look of exhaustion consumes me most Friday nights. So I'll laugh and take another sip of my beer and just try to slosh, ya know. Relax and transpire.

DNA

When he was 10 months and 24 days old, Erik Lund Neumann became my first student. At that point, he already knew about our life together; he'd been alive longer. "Hey Rye," he'll say now, "you know what I be when I grow up?" It's always a difficult moment for me, but over the years, my response has become almost reflexive...I try to say what seems right, which is to say, I try to say what seems normal, "I don't know. What do you want to be?" And then I wait to hear the answers I've heard so many times before. A professional bowler. A journalist. Married. Someday, I hope Erik becomes all of those things. I hope that I can help him become all of those things. After all, that's why I was born. But here I want to pretend we are both grown-ups. I want to pretend Erik does not have Down Syndrome. I want to tell him what I've buried in the recesses of my mind, what the whole tattoo business on my left arm means, and then I want to say to him that he will be all of those things when he grows up. This is what I can't seem to forget:

He is a short, muscular man of about thirty. There are times when I've been afraid of him--afraid of something--and sometimes when I am dreaming, there are times when the night is beyond black, and we are trying, desperately, to escape the end of the world. We are running through the backyards that are familiar to us, distinct landscapes indicative of the places we have known, and invariably there is a moment when there is nowhere else to run and our lives fade to black.

But to backtrack, I never thought I'd get a tattoo. Shortly after midday, before the most recent of new years, I drove onto a friend's driveway inside the neighborhood we grew up in. All of his equipment was in the kitchen, spread out along a wide wooden table, mingling with the sunlight, and for 3 hours we talked about the double helix tattoo design and life and all that had happened since high school. We were working together--one man asking questions while the other answered--and I remember being jittery from all the coffee I drank before it officially began. The basement was familiar and cold. For the first few moments I didn't know what to think, not sure about the significance of my choice, wondering how I would explain this symbol in a way that makes sense.

Down Syndrome occurs when an individual has three, rather than two, copies of the 21st chromosome. This additional genetic material altered the course of Erik's development, and, in a slightly different way, altered the course of my development as well. Deoxyribonucleic acid, also known as DNA, is like, this thing called a nucleic acid...hence the whole "acid" part. The reason it is important to know about this whole nucleic acid thing is because it is within this acid that the genetic instructions, kind of like blueprints, used in the development and functioning of all living things, can be found. More often than not, the double helix is used to represent this DNA structure.

6 months before the tattoo I was on a plane to visit my sister in Oregon. Her name is Kali and she knew that I had all but given up drawing, so she was surprised to hear that I'd been working on a tattoo design. I don't know what it was about that particular night, but when I reached out with my pencil and drew three X's in the middle of this double helix sketch I'd been working on, something just seemed to click. The lines had been drawn lightly in case there was a sudden need for impulsive erasing. And then for maybe half an hour I sat there and just stared at the page. Very gradually, in tiny slivers, I began to shade the wavy border of the structure. When I was done, it felt like a simple enough solution. 21 straight lines to represent the 21st chromosome. Three X's to signify the three, rather than two, copies of that very chromosome. The blueprints used in the development and functioning of my life.

When we were younger, the rage I kept inside was fierce. I remember bottling everything up, wondering if I was always going to have this misplaced anger, wondering if I would ever figure out why, wondering if I needed to open up and just talk to someone, then thinking it was a bad idea, and then waking up one morning and feeling like I just came out of this thick fog.

In the dream Erik is always wearing a gray t-shirt with an orange 5 ball dead center, black gym shorts, and a Fossil wristwatch. His shoulders are slightly lowered, his head turned to the left as if listening to the second hand take time away. He seems preoccupied with something. He wears the watch on his left wrist, time facing the flat black sky, moving in a way that suggests there is somewhere we need to be soon. There's never any sound--just this impending feeling of doom. In a weird sort of way, it almost seems like Erik is an extension of his watch, or my abstracted mind, but there is also this realness to what is happening...I can feel it with the increasing rate of my heart. I had already pulled the gate open to our neighbor's backyard. I ushered Erik through first and came up out of a crouch to close the gate and continued running behind him. It was almost automatic...like we'd been running for years, in and out of people's lives...so much so that it didn't even faze us.

I did not hate getting a tattoo; I did not see myself as one committing a sin, I did not contemplate ideals with any sort of heft, nor did I dwell of the meanings of truth or life. I sat down in a chair that lived in this cold and familiar basement from my youth and tried to stay still. I tried to focus on the conversation I was having with an old friend, and tried to really listen, because so often that can be the most challenging thing to do. I was nervous yet excited. There were no thoughts of regret. The tattoo utensils were to make something permanent—an idea that I had been trying for so long to not let define me, but in such an attempt, it seems that at certain points in my life I had been using the very idea to destroy me. So I leaned back in the chair and stared out into a backyard I knew well and felt my mind retreat into a dream that has been rehashed time and time again.

Erik had already started running before I told him to run. The backyard was full of barren trees and pine straw disguised the uneven footing of the terrain we were attempting to cover. We had to find someplace to hide, but the basement doors were locked and I had nothing to throw, and I remember this light that came shining from behind me, like the flash on a camera had clicked, and I remember falling down and not being able to get back up right away. The light bounced off the single paned windows and I turned around to look for Erik. I did not see him, but he had to have been somewhere because I saw his watch on the ground not far from where I had fallen, just two or three feet away, then I paused, glaring up into the night, and looked back down at the watch and tried to cover my mouth but never did. It occurred to me then that I was about to die. If only I would have known, I could have warned him. The light pushed me backwards—not gently but harshly—I wasn't ready for it—and I felt my body jerk upward like I'd just been revived by a defibrillator. I fell back into the basement chair. The rubber gloves my buddy was wearing were off. He was looking at the finished tattoo, his head kind of tilted as if he were evaluating the effort, his arms, covered with full sleeves of tattoos, folded one over the other.

"Whadda you think?" he said.

I think the idea is now something else. Something less fleeting. Something more prominent. The only thing I've left to do, really, is find my direction...find out what it all really means...to me.

For the longest time, I don't know that it's every really been a question of what Erik can or cannot do. Based on the limited amount of life I've had to experience, I'd venture to say you can do almost anything you set your mind to. There will always be "what if" scenarios and opportunities that pass us by. It's always going to be that way...but I suppose it is up to the individual to use the information at hand to make the best decision possible.

A few months ago, I remember, I was having dinner with another friend who is much smarter than myself. After a couple drinks we started talking somewhat philosophically about my thoughts on Erik and our relationship. He asked me simple questions that for some reason, just seemed far too complicated to answer. I couldn't' find the words. Got me thinking though...what if things were reversed? What if I had Down Syndrome and not Erik? What if I could ask him that question? What would that conversation be like? Would I even be able to make it through a conversation like that?

Perhaps it doesn't matter, or rather...perhaps it shouldn't matter. Maybe I think about this stuff too much. But then again, maybe that's why I need to write this. Even now I haven't finished sorting everything out. I doubt that I ever will. In the classroom ya know, it's different. When I'm trying to teach, I can escape these heavier things and get lost in the fog I was familiar with during high school. That's also part of the problem...some kind of denial I guess. That's why here, now, I will pretend that Erik and I are grown-ups. I will pretend that he does not have Down Syndrome and after I have said everything I can think to say, I will tell him he will be all of those things when he grows up...and then, I will help him.

He is a short, muscular man of about thirty. There are times when I've been afraid of him--afraid of something--and sometimes when I am dreaming, he is sitting across from me at the kitchen table, like we've been there for hours. A half-eaten pizza ornaments the rectangular table I've had since college. Empty Diet Coke cans and Sweetwater bottles loiter around our forearms which rest casually on both ends of the table. He is waiting for me to say something.

Erik, I...worry. I worry about you. I worry about your happiness, and wonder if, in some...sort of way we are depriving you of that pursuit. Sometimes I think about how it might have been. Maybe we would have all hung out in the neighborhood together. Maybe you would have been this superstar football player or insanely brilliant mathematician.

It's not that I don't understand you, but I think sometimes you get frustrated because you can't put all your thoughts into words. And then I'll think about what I just said and realize it's true for all of us. We all struggle with miscommunication but I've been taught to see it differently.

I've been taught to view your inability as something that is not normal, as something that is an unfortunate difference from my inability and I hate myself for that.

It's not that I don't want you to be you, because without you, I would not be me in the way that I am, or was...I just, shit...shit, I think for the longest time I didn't want you to see yourself as someone who is not like the rest of us...and that sounds fucking awful, but I don't know how else to say it. Like, I remember when I started college at App, and Mom was telling me about the homecoming dance you went to. She was telling me how you wanted to dance with girls that night, but you didn't want to dance with the girls from your class, you wanted to dance with the pretty girls ya know, the ones on Homecoming Court and even though she didn't say it, I knew what she meant. For the first time it really hit me. I knew then that you saw a difference between the girls in your class, which meant that you were aware of this difference in yourself, and even now as I retell it, it's hard for me not to lose it.

When were in school, after we moved to Georgia, I didn't want to be at home all the time because it seemed like things would only be the way you wanted them to be. Which for me, was kind of like you saying you only wanted me the way you wanted me. That's part of why I needed to get so far away after high school. I needed those 300 miles...I needed that distance and even though, at the time, I probably wouldn't have admitted it, I was hoping for the best. I was hoping to become a better person. I want you to be able to tell everyone what you want them to hear. You know, you're the reason why I was born. That little nugget of information is something I've been grappling with for nearly a decade. And as we are getting older, and I suppose, as thoughts of mortality seem to be creeping into my daily life, I wonder if our fates will forever be intertwined? I wonder about Mom and Dad. I wonder how this has affected and effected Kali. I wonder if you will develop Alzheimer's and I wonder how long you're going to live. I wonder if that's weird...ya know, like, yeah, I do think about death...my own death, but I don't dwell on it too much. If I'm being completely honest, I actually lose more sleep over yours.

It's like, what the hell...I feel like there are certain things I can teach you, and talk to you about, and help you with, and protect you from, but death...what the hell can I do about that? And what if I go first? Sounds so fucking morbid but I feel like the older we get, and the more friends and family that I see become the departed, the more this shit starts flooding my head. Will you be the reason why I'm gone and you're still here? Will I be the reason you're gone and I'm still here?

As close as I as we've become as brothers, I don't think our relationship is the same for you as it is for me...not that it should be, but for whatever narcissistic reason, I feel like my side of our relationship brings with it more...depth.

I can't believe I just said that.

I'm such an asshole.

We can head out the door to go any number of places...we have, and I don't know if you've ever really noticed this because I try very hard to hide it, but my defenses are up. Like, Amber alert and then some. Truth is, I am so overly protective and perhaps overly sensitive to the way anyone looks at you or treats you that most of the time, if someone doesn't understand you, or if it seems to me like they don't hear you or are looking at you in weird way, I want to rip their fucking head off. I envision their destruction. That's how messed up I am about all of this. I feel like I'm supposed to protect you from...from, harm, injustice, wrongdoing...I don't know, and the American way.

I feel like I'm supposed to be a superhero.

We both know the reason why I'm no longer at home and you're still there. But I just want you to know, if you ever want to leave, I can help you. I will help you. Home is great though, don't get me wrong. Mom and Dad are the greatest parents anyone could ever ask for. I guess I just want you to know you are capable of great things. You should do great things. You will do great things. So many of the kids I teach squander their potential on stupid shit. I don't want that to be you. I won't let that be you. You and I, we are very much an extension of one another. The corny thing to say would be that we complete each other, but in truth, I think we complement each other.

You've always been good at stealing the show which made it pretty easy for me to cover my tracks. You've always inspired me to be good and I hope I've done the same for you. As brothers, you and I have experienced things that other brothers have not. I have more regrets about things I've thought and done in relation to you then I care to mention, so I won't...I'll just say that for the longest time, I've let that regret transform itself into this blackness that's been pouring into a bottomless cup, flooding my mind.

I spilled those regrets when I got this tattoo. It is very much about you and I. It's about intertwining fates. It's a reminder why we both exist. But you know what, it's also a reminder that you still have a lot to teach me, and I, in return, have a tremendous amount to teach you.

You will be a professional bowler.

You will be a journalist.

You will get married.

I will help you.

So...older brother, raise your Diet Coke and I'll raise my Sweetwater.

Here's to learning about life...together, until death do us part.

HEADBUTT

I don't recall many of the great classes, or even great students, I've had, strange as it may seem, but I can relive some of the more remarkable transgressions of my teaching career with the kind of clarity that is, at times unnerving. Every semester I've been a teacher there has been at least one student whose sole purpose in life was to make me regret that one, seemingly insignificant, moment in time when I decided to become a teacher.

"Gotu all wrapped up an you canteedin do shhiittt, Neumann!"

Deshawd Jackson was one of those students.

Common sense will tell you, especially in the era of smart phones and YouTube, even if you're not in the wrong, never touch a student. Never. Interestingly enough, teaching will tell you, in lieu of many other things, sense is not always common.

Deshawd Jackson, who was infamous for his loud mouth and angelic smile, decided to test me one afternoon. After being suspended for two weeks he strolled through the doorway to Room 300 nonchalantly; well after the tardy bell rang. I'd already taken attendance and somehow managed to get my small cluster of derelicts started on the warm-up when Deshawd made his presence known.

Deshawd = Wat up nigga!

I could have ignored him. I could have ignored what he said. Just let him sit down and try to keep the unexpected productivity of that day's class going. Unfortunately, I knew his peers were waiting and assessing. Why do we have to go get tardy passes when we're late but Deshawd can just walk into class after the bell, say what he said, and just take a seat? They'd be right and ya know what, I'd agree with them, but at the same time, I can't stand it when a situation that should be nothing, turns into something.

I looked at Deshawd, then at the class, then at Deshawd again. I remember struggling to decide how to approach the situation. Do I talk to Deshawd privately in the hallway and risk losing the attention of the entire class? or do I address the situation with Deshawd so that all can hear, giving Deshawd an audience to boost his defiant confidence? The first question would almost guarantee a better diffusion of potential badness. The second question implies a lack of confidentiality and consequently, a greater possibility for trouble. Either way, I've got to do something. In the hopes of neutralizing Deshawd's impact, I met him at the classroom door and was about to escort him into the hallway for a refresher on classroom etiquette when he picked me up and said,

"Gotu all wrapped up an you canteedin do shhiittt, Neumann!"

Deshawd...put. me. down.

Aha! Ha! Why? Watshu gonna do Neumann?

I have absolutely no idea. They didn't cover teacher-student altercations at the New Teacher Institute.

I swivel my head to the right. Deshawd's pupils follow mine.

U gonna press the white call button? It ain dat serious. How you gonna do dat anyway Neumann?...gotu all wrapped up an you canteedin do shhiittt.

It would appear so.

Ryan, stay calm. Maintain.

Deshawd...this is the last time I'm going to ask politely...please. put. me. down.

Deshawd turns his head to address the rest of "my" class. 13 or so young men who have earned little to no English credit in high school. Some are sophomores. Some should be seniors. Some should have graduated already.

Listen da this nigga!..Aha! Ha! (takes a moment to clear his throat)...Neumann. no. I. will. not. put. you. down...(in his best white guy voice)

The other boys begin laughing uncontrollably as Deshawd, who is holding me in a bear hug two inches off the ground, sways from left to right as if to illustrate to his fellow classmates, as well as to me, that he is in complete control of the situation. I glance out the corner of my eye. The classroom door is closed. Wonderful. Bobble head to the right. The white call button, to be used in emergency situations only, seems miles away. Fantastic. I redirect my line of sight so that Deshawd and I are looking at each other. He's grinning from ear-to-ear while emitting a chuckle through clenched teeth. I can smell the Hot Cheetos on his breath. Fluorescent ceiling lights reflect in pupils that appear devoid of compassion.

Me = ...Deshawd...

Hahaha!...Neumann, I ain leddin you down so stop askin. Eh! (He motions with a head nod)...somebody check Neumann's computer bag and see if der's anything good in der.

Soooo, wait. Is this really happening? Am I going to let this happen? Ryan, think about it. A, you're in a bear hug. B, no authority figures are even remotely nearby to help you. C, you're about to be robbed. Great. What did Hacker always use to say? Lead with the top of the forehead? I think so. Are you really gonna do this? A student, Deshawd, has you detained while other students are about to raid your computer bag. Do I have any other options? I could yell for help. I've never been much of a yeller though. Ah screw it.

Insert headbutt here.

Deshawd = OWWwww! Fuck Neumann!

Deshawd's bear hug is broken. He does a backward stagger into a table where he promptly sits down grumbling. I do a uniform check. Jacket's a little messed up. Tie is probably crooked but that's normal.

I's only kiddin Neumann! Damn!

13 or so young men are no longer laughing but quietly taking their seats. I fix the collar on my jacket while doing a visual inspection of my technological belongings.

Everything appears intact, but I make sure before saying another word to Deshawd, who is already grinning again.

Deshawd, it was only a love tap, don't be so dramatic man. You're not even bleeding. You could have just put me down and none of this would have been necessary. Why can't you just let me do my job?

Deshawd = (one hand on his nose for dramatic effect) Dat ain't no fun.

Fun? Seriously?

You lucky Neumann.

He says with adolescent authority.

Lucky? Really? Why is that?

You lucky I ain bleedin...cuz den I'd really have to fuck you up.

Me = (insert rolling eyes) That's great. Maybe next time, alright. I need you to get out some paper so we can get started with class.

I ain got no paper...must be trippin.

I feel deflated. I let out a deep sigh and my shoulders drop.

Alright man, look, I already gave out all my spare paper for today. Anyone in here wanna give Deshawd some paper?

Look around the room and I can tell I've already lost them. If we don't get started within the first 15 minutes of class, this group is a lost cause. Some have their heads down. Some are texting, playing video games on their PSWhatever, drawing, or finding some other way to escape the reality of this seemingly destitute situation.

No one heard my question.

Alright Deshawd, let me see if there's some scrap paper in the English office. I'll be back in a minute. Keep the door open.

I walk out of Room 300 leaving the door wide and gaping. Make my way down the hallway as fast as I can without running. Not even 15 steps removed there is a calamitous

BOOM!
    BOOM!
        BOOM!
            ...BOOM!
                Owwwwuuuch!
That hurt. Where the hell ...what is that noi...oh, right.

Hollow boxcars berate the train tracks of downtown Atlanta while its gentrified tenants sleep. The boom boom boom of boxcars colliding with one another at interchanging velocities echoes through the night with an understood regularity. Machinery that is both animate and inanimate facilitates the movement of supply and demand while the thunderous friction of opposing forces rattles the antique window panes.

We don't have any furniture yet...Mara and I, that is. We just bought this loft downtown in an old warehouse district; used to be a super unsafe neighborhood and now it's just moderately unsafe. So, ya know, cars getting broken into, people being held up at night and I guess during the day too, homeless folk wondering about in varying states of consciousness. That's the trade-off for wanting to be hip and urban though.

I was sleeping in two folding chairs until that train just came barreling through. Sometimes falling down can be fun. Tonight it's not. Laying in sawdust on uneven stacks of 2 X 4's isn't my ideal bed, but I'm tired and don't feel like moving. I close my eyes and hope that exhaustion will once again give way to a stress-related coma. A few minutes pass and another train enters the city. Couple that with paint fumes from the work Mara's stepbrother was doing earlier, and sleep becomes a fleeting memory.

Too much noise, all this locomotive commotion and I...can't stop thinking about yesterday.

Did that really happen?

My hands are now resting on the bathroom sink. Questions of morality.

Did that really fucking happen? Was that me?

My eyes open and my head flings up. (Insert reflective stare down.) I get the impression the stranger staring back at me is thinking the same thing.

Mirror = Ryan, I'm not angry. I'm just...it's just...I'm disappointed. You shouldn't be headbutting people; especially students. Stuff like that could cost you your job.

Sometimes, I am my mother.

I put our hands together and contemplate the possibility of prayer. It's a fleeting notion. My hands break the Amen position and I open the medicine cabinet.

"Writing is a solitary existence. Do you exist today?"

That question has been posted on the inside of my medicine cabinet for the better part of a year now.

Do I exist?

I close the cabinet for further reflection.

No.

Exit the bathroom stage right and walk round into the kitchen.
Stranded in this empty house; floor is concrete cold. Hardwood floors
crackle with each weary step. As I glance into an open bedroom I see a
space that is dark and lifeless. She's working on another deadline.

Driven by the stranglehold of the previous afternoon I stagger towards
the refrigerator. Open the door to examine our meager collection of
edibles. Water, milk, bread, beer, some leftover wings from last night
and...wait, beer.

Close the door. What time is it?
                              5:00AM.
                                    Shit.
                                          Work in 3 hours.
It's only Wednesday. The door remains closed.

I don't think I can do this. I'm not even teaching anymore. I
mean...shit, I headbutt a person yesterday. Not even! I headbutt a
student. I've never headbutt anyone in my entire life and I decide to
start with a student? Fucking brilliant, Ryan.

I fucking hate this! This isn't what I want to do with my life. I don't
wanna be some damn teacher who spends 30 years in the system only
to end up as some weathered, borderline senior citizen well versed in
cynical bitching.

DAMN IT!
          What...the...fuck.
                    Open the fridge.
                              Open a beer.
                                    Drink beer.
Empty beer. No wait, empty, beer. 5:10 AM

Congratulations Ryan! You've just reached a record low in your life.

Well done.

One beer down on a Wednesday morning. Should probably eat something. Not really that hungry. Grab the leftover wings and commence binge eating. Crack open another beer.

By 6:00AM I've abandoned all hope, taken a shower, and am halfway done with my 3rd beer when I get a text message.

Flip phone = up and open.

1 New Message. View.

It's DJ.

Reading is unnecessary. I know exactly why I've been summoned.

DJ = Neumann, can I get a ride to school I know this is last minute I'm at my aunts thanks.

Yeah man, you know the drill. Be ready for pickup by 7:00.

This isn't our first rodeo.

DJ was the first student to adopt me as a surrogate...we'll say, supportive figure in life. His mom and dad have been kind of, absent at various points during his high school career. I don't mean to imply that I fill in for them by any means, but, more than often than not, I'll drive him to and from school. You know, stuff like that.

Cool beans. Thanks so much Neumann.

No problem, man.

6:10AM.

Time to be responsible.

JUNO

I do not see how a movie with profanity, sexual innuendos, discussion about sex, talks of abortion, and the female character going to get an abortion counts as a lesson plan.

This too is real. Teaching can save us. I'm 28 years old, and I've been a high school english teacher for five years now, so I've learned to take certain things with a grain of salt, but even still, at this very moment, I keep dreaming that email alive. That one statement reply. The text messages. My colleagues' expressions...their comments. The unexplainable yet inescapable feeling of guilt.

Can I let myself forget?

That's really what it boils down to. Can I let myself forget what was said? Can I let myself forget what they made me do? Can I let myself forget what I've become? In response to all four of those questions, I can tell you without hesitation the answer is no. And what that answer translates to, or rather, what it transforms itself into, is a swelling rage.

But in this story, which is kind of like trying to remember a dream, the rage becomes a fuel...a fuel facilitating words onto a white blank page.

Begin here: a refrigerator heater breaks. On an afternoon in early March 2011, I opened up our stainless steel appliance to find lukewarm milk, defrosted chicken, and mushy peas. It only took a minute or two, and the thought of a day off sounded more than good, but even so, I had to get on the computer that night and order up a substitute teacher. For the next half hour I worked on sub plans. It was a mash-up endeavor, like early rap rock, and the movie Juno was going to be my bridge. When I was finished, I set the alarm an hour early so I'd have time to photocopy handouts the next morning. It was all good intentions. I remember the potential; I remember Twain and a lesson on humorists and heaps of current issues on teen pregnancy that would make for great writing prompts. Wrote an email to my co-teacher so she'd know what to expect.

Decided to go with JUNO for today's movie selection. I made a handout for our students that explains why they will be viewing the beginning of that movie today.

But basically, I was looking at the 2 episodes of the World of Jenks that we have coming up and noticed they are both centering around the goals and aspirations of young women. So, I was thinking that in addition to the normal story map material, we could also do a compare and contrast activity between JUNO and the World of Jenks episodes. There's a connection to all of this too...it'll be with Twain and some current issues and what not but I don't want to ramble on.

Hope you're able to go hiking this weekend and I'll give you all the details on Monday!

-Ryan

Little did I know, this simple, seemingly innocuous plan, would propel an imminent exodus from the school I never thought I'd leave.

The Sears repair man arrived earlier than expected that day. He'd previously established a working window from 12 to 4. Needless to say, I was little surprised when I got a call from the front gate shortly after 11 that morning. The malfunctioning freezer was an easy fix. Sears Man might have been working for an hour. Guess broken heaters aren't that hard to replace; especially when the service rep has extras in the back of his truck.

As I'm making small talk with the dreadlocked repair man, my school phone beeps to announce that I've just received a text message. I ignore it so as not to seem like one of those people enslaved to technology and the immediacy of information. A few minutes later, it beeps again. Then about a minute after the second text, the Bat phone beeps once more.

What the hell?

I excuse myself and grab the phone.

3 New Text Messages.

Message 1 = neumann! why did mr moline stop the movie, turn on the lights, and storm out of the classroom?

Mr. Moline is the relatively new Principal of the school I worked for.

Shit.

The second and third messages are similar...alarmingly similar.

At the beginning of each new semester, I give students my cell phone number in case they need to contact me regarding assignments, questions about assignments, or various unexpected happenings. I suppose it's safe to say that these messages, all from students, would fall in the "unexpected" category.

Suddenly panicked, I turn on my county issued laptop and login to the district email. Rapidly searching the inbox for something that could dispel the overwhelming anxiety that is taking over my being, there is one email that stands out almost immediately...an email from my co-teacher.

From: Liza Klein

To: Ryan Neumann

Subject: Re: Movie Selection

3.4.2011 (Friday) 12:04 PM

Mr. Moline is observing today...................... I hope Juno is safe :(He is in here now.

I sent the following reply at 12:16 PM.

Hey!

I would think so...it's rated PG-13.

4 minutes later.

It's not safe. He demanded the movie to be turned off and he stormed out. Not good.

At that point, my heart dropped into my stomach. It was Liza's first year teaching at my school. Per, whatever kind of protocol, all first year teachers are observed by the Principal for their annual performance evaluation. Today just happened to be hers.

At 12:23 PM, I sent the following...

I know I'm not at school but, is there anything I can do?

The passing of each minute thereafter felt like an eternity. Unsure of what to do, I decided to compose an email to Mr. Moline.

Good Afternoon Mr. Moline,

I am sure that by now, you are aware that I am not at school today, but I did want to contact you and say that I know my substitute teacher plans have been vetoed for the day which I can wholeheartedly accept. I suppose the main point of this email is just to let you know that I will accept whatever consequences you deem appropriate concerning this matter.

I am absent today because of a broken refrigerator at my house. Should you need to speak with me at any point, I will be happy to make myself available at any time. I apologize for any unneeded stress and/or confusion I may have caused.

Ryan Neumann

Literally a minute after I sent that message, Liza sent me a suggestion.

I think you should e-mail Mr. Moline.

I felt uncomfortable, though I LOVE the movie... professionally, I knew that we should not watch it.

Couple of questions... Was Juno on the waiver list and did the parents sign it? If not, we need to send a letter out Monday explaining that Juno was played and explain why.

Okay.

I just sent Mr. Moline an email.

I'll have a letter ready for Monday.

I'm really sorry, this is about the last thing I would have wanted to happen.

It's okay. I don't know what's going to happen with my observation but whatever will be, will be. Let's get those letters out asap Monday. I told Mr. Moline that you had an assignment prepared.

I will see you Monday.

At home, I felt nauseous. Do I wait until Monday to get this resolved? Can I wait that long? Why hasn't Mr. Moline replied to my email? There's no way I'm getting fired over this. I mean, right? For showing Juno? No way.

At approximately 1:11 PM on March 4th, 2011, Mr. Moline sent me a reply.

Mr. Neumann

I do not see how a movie with profanity, sexual innuendos, discussion about sex, talks of abortion, and the female character going to get an abortion counts as a lesson plan.

Obviously, he hadn't seen the movie before.

Aside from a broken fridge, I had a flight to catch that day. My flight to Austin, Texas was due to depart from Atlanta in the early evening, and if you've ever been in, through, or at the Atlanta airport, then you probably know you can't just show up 30 minutes before your flight. You plan ahead. Allow yourself time to navigate the oceans of semi-civil stupidity.

Do I have time for this? Is this worth potentially missing my flight for?

Yes.

I decided I had to get this misunderstanding resolved, so I got in my car and completed the 20 mile daily commute to my place of employment in record time. Parked in my usual spot along the outskirts of the student lot. Made sure the cell phones were on silent. Walking into school, I imagined all the different ways this conversation could go. I envisioned all the explaining and defending I would need to do so that Mr. Moline would see, clearly, how brilliant of a lesson plan this was...that I was not simply showing a movie because I was absent, but that there was in fact, some genuine outside-of-the-box thinking going on here. I'd have to watch my tone, I thought. Don't want to be too sarcastic or heaven forbid, too opinionated with the boss man. Need to remain indifferent, I thought.

Opening the door to the front office, I politely said hello to the student aides running the front desk and made my way to the school secretary. Without saying a word, I could tell by the way she looked at me, she already knew.

"Good Afternoon Ms. Webster, is Mr. Moline accepting...visitors this afternoon?"

Ms. Webster's desk is in plain view of Mr. Moline's office. On this particular afternoon, his door was open. I could see him typing on his keyboard. But the thing about Mr. Moline is, or was, you can't just walk into his realm. You must have an appointment.

I did not have an appointment.

Ms. Webster, who had always been nothing but kind to me, got up from her chair. She told me she was not sure, but she would go check for me. As Ms. Webster walked the 15 feet to Mr. Moline's doorway I could hear her say, "Mr. Moline, Ryan Neumann is here to see you. Do you have a minute?"

When Ms. Webster returned to her seat, I had my answer.

He's busy right now. He said you will have to come back later, sorry.

Seriously?

I have nowhere to go. Class is taken care of. I could try to find my co-teacher but I have absolutely no idea where she is. Our class had been over for about 20 minutes at that point which meant there was only a substitute up in Room 300. The students were probably doing nothing, and while normally that's something that would bother me, sitting there in the Principal's office, or rather, outside the Principal's office, it was probably the furthest thing from my mind.

Having nowhere to go, I chose to wait. The time was nearing 2:30 PM. I'd thrown my backpack full of clothes for the weekend in the back of my car just in case there was a need to haul ass to the airport from school. 5 minutes passed...then 10...then 20...and as the clock was nearing 3:00 PM, Ms. Webster appeared before me.

For 25 minutes I'd sat in disbelief. Am I really waiting in the Principal's office right now? Like, this is for real? Can't believe it. Seems so ironic. Teacher man sitting in the Principal's office waiting to be reprimanded. Had to become a teacher before I ever got reprimanded in school. Never in my life would I have thought...ah, whatever.

When Ms. Webster appeared before me I was in a daze.

Mr. Moline just got off the phone and has a minute before his next meeting, so he can probably see you if you get in there quick.

I could tell she was trying to help me but in the back of my head I was thinking, "great, a whole minute, this should be perfect."

Upon entering Mr. Moline's office, I wasn't sure what to say at first. I felt like projectile vomiting explanations but that didn't seem appropriate. Mr. Moline's face was buried in paperwork. He didn't even raise his head to look at me until I was a few feet away from his desk. Decided to go with a casual greeting. Rules of etiquette and all that. Can't go wrong with a good ole hello.

Hello.

Hello Mr. Neumann.

About midway through an extremely awkward pause Mr. Moline started to speak.

He had no questions for me. He did not want to know what I was thinking, nor was he interested in hearing what I had to say. He was on a strictly regimented schedule. This was not the time for diatribe. Our conversation, if you can call it that, lasted all of 2 minutes.

It was a very informative 2 minutes. I learned a lot.

Quickly, almost instantaneously, I learned this was not at all how I'd imagined the conversation going.

I learned that my choice of Juno was the wrong choice.

I learned that a memo would be placed in my file concerning this incident so that, in the event of a parental complaint, the school, as well as myself, would be covered.

I learned that even if I chose to speak to this man, he would not be listening.

I learned that I could not talk to this man.

Throughout the course of this brief exchange, my answers were short, respectful, and in no particular order.

Yes. Yes. I understand. Right. Yes, sir. No. Yes. Ok. Yes. Thanks. Have a good afternoon.

Mr. Moline's dictation ended on a cordial note. He knew I had things to take care of, and didn't want to waste too much of my time. Really. He said if there was anything else we needed to talk about, we could talk about it on Monday.

I left his office dazed and confused. I couldn't feel my legs. Unlocking the driver's side door to my car, I'd almost no recollection of how I got there. I felt weightless. Did I float?

I made it to the Atlanta airport in plenty of time. Spent the weekend in Austin with some old college friends and tried my best to sink the betrayal, guilt, remorse, and shrinking sense of self-worth I felt beneath a sea of alcohol. Did a pretty good job of it too. Sometimes it's fun to travel back in time...to go swimming with immaturity. Go back to a place when you were just discovering yourself. Discovering what you wanted. What was important to you. What kind of person you thought you were. What kind of person you thought you wanted to be. Sitting in the Austin airport that Sunday afternoon, I found myself slowly floating back to the surface. The closer I got, the more I thought about school the next day. What would it be like? Who would know?

What about that letter? I told Liza I'd have an explanatory letter when I got back...I haven't even started.

By the time I got back to Atlanta, I'd all but arrived on the shore of sobriety. Thinking clearly for the first time in days, there was this...irritating sensation. In fact, it was so irritating, and became so persistent, that it almost felt like it was consuming me. No longer filled with doubts about my reasons for choosing Juno, nor about my competencies as a teacher, I just felt...angry. Angry about everything. Like, I know this guy is my boss, well not only that, he is the Principal of the school I work for, but he totally overreacted. What kind of example is he setting? Storming out of the classroom. Why the hell am I getting reprimanded for something that I was not even...stop. Stop it, Ryan. Sometimes it's too easy to be thinking those thoughts. It's easy to play the blame game.

I still had a job to do. I had a letter to write...some sort of explanation to give my students.

Concluding it would be best to get some sleep, I woke early the next day. Hours before the sun would even attempt to stretch its fingers atop the Atlanta skyline, I made some coffee, turned on my computer, and began to write.

From: Neumann

To: Neumann's Students

American Literature Blocks 2, 3, 4

7 March 2011

Apologia

I am sorry. I, am sorry. I...am sorry. I am...sorry. I am, sorry. I am, ~~sorry~~. Think I like that last one the best. Yeaaahhhh...for sure, let's hold off on that whole sorry business for the moment. I am...ready, I think. No wait, I think, therefore I am... ready. Yes. Winner. Okay, we shall proceed. The title of this paper looks very similar to the word *apology*, and that, in light of a more recent history I promise you, is no coincidence.

According to *The Oxford English Dictionary*, an apology is, "an explanation that can be offered to a person affected by one's actions that no offense was intended." For instance, if you (student) were affected by my selection of Juno (□action) this past Friday (3.4.2011), I (Neumann) could explain my reasons for choosing the previously mentioned film as I did not intend, or have it in mind, that my actions would offend you. Seems to me that's usually the way apologies go. Something bad happens, or someone is offended, and someone apologizes. Someone always apologizes...even if they're not wholeheartedly apologetic...even if they're not sorry.

The letter went on. By the time I was done, it was nearly 2 pages in length. But something happened while I was writing. I realized I did not want to be at my school anymore. I realized that I can do better than this...whatever this was. I decided this Juno event, however insignificant, would be the last straw of sorts. I could and would forgive, but I would not forget...not for a second.

For the most part, I tried to carry myself with composure, a kind of casual poise, during the last 3 months of this most recent school year. However, every once and awhile, there were times of frustration, when I would quit or wanted to quit but couldn't, when the expressions on my students' faces grew solemn because they just wanted to be done with this class already. Didn't matter if I had this really cool creative lesson or if it was busy work, they just didn't care. It got worse after Spring Break. Six weeks left in the semester and everyone's gone. Teachers, students, administrators...we're all the walking dead. And the thing about it is, it never used to get to me. Like, I was impervious to this apathy thing. But something had happened this past year, something I could not define. I don't know, it all just seemed so different.

One afternoon, so close to the end of the school year, all the apathy and bullshit finally got to me. Seniors are allowed to take their final exams early. That way they can prepare for, and practice for, the graduation ceremony during the last full week of school. I had a few seniors in all of my classes this past semester. Repeat offenders who hadn't passed American Literature when they were juniors. As per usual, I was standing by the door to Room 300. Greeting everyone as they walked in, this one student, a senior with a...shall we say vibrant personality, looks at me and says, "I'm sooooo over this fucking class."

She said it in undertones. She said it in a way that wasn't meant for me to hear. Fortunately for me though, the past 5 years have facilitated a keen ear for shit talking. Close your eyes. Let it go, Ryan. Just let it go. For reasons that I cannot put into words, I did. I let it go. I figured, it's my last day with this girl, just let her take the final and get out of here. Besides, it's not like I can grade her on behavior...although, I mean, doesn't behavior in some cases determine what a student....

nevermind.

She took her final and class ended. The bell rings to signal the end of the school day and I sit down to check email. One of my "job expectations." Checking email at least once before school, and once after school. So here we are, after school, and I notice an email from the administrator over my department. She needs me to stop by to sign the paperwork for my annual performance evaluation. Thinking nothing of it, I walk down to her office where she is surprisingly, if not superficially, happy to see me. We sit down at her conference table and she goes over my markings. A sprawling format of emergence which for teachers, kind of means mediocre middle-of-the-road. So, emerging here. Emerging there. No Proficient marks anywhere. As we approach the end of formal explaining, I try to hide my genuine lack of surprise and act interested. We've already had this conversation. We had it weeks ago. Old news. Then she gets to a portion that has been altered. I was marked down in one category from Emerging to whatever is the lower mark, or actually, to whatever label is the lowest mark. I was told it was because of the Juno incident...because of an incident I was not actually at school teaching for. She asked me if I understood.

I'm not sure if irritation, or even resentment, has a flavor, but hearing that I was devaluated at a level below that of even the most moderate satisfaction I don't know, I could taste it. Like I'd been cut and was now tasting my own blood. Marked down for what had happened when I was not present.

Oh yes, of course. I understand.

It didn't matter. I was done. Gone. A mere shell of a teacher. We arrived at the back page, the page in need of acknowledgment signatures. It had already been presigned by the Principal and the administrator I was speaking with. Protocol dictates that these signatures, or at least the Principal's, should be added after the teacher has signed his or her annual performance evaluation. That way, if revisions are made to the form, or if a teacher does not agree with all of the evaluation, the form can be discussed, changed, and then presented before the Principal for final...approval. This was not the case for me. I later found out this what not the case for others as well. I signed it and was told I would receive a copy to keep for my records.

I never did.

I felt like I was going to explode. Exiting the administrator's office, I passed my classroom and headed directly for the men's faculty restroom. Needed someplace to lock the anger in. Someplace without windows.

I'm sooooo over this fucking class. Her words had infected me.

Close your eyes. Let it go, Ryan. Just let it go.

Standing in the men's faculty restroom, I was looking at myself in the mirror when I noticed that down in the right-hand corner a student, it had to have been a student, had written "FUCK YOU!" in black sharpie. That's when enough was finally enough.

All this pent up frustration. I had to get rid of it. It was like watching a movie...like watching a character...like watching Edward Norton in the **25ᵗʰ Hour**.

Neumann: (looking into the mirror, deep sigh, cracking of knuckles) You know what, fuck you, too.

Mirror: Excuse me? What was that?...Fuck me? Nah, fuck you Neumann, or Ryan, fuck you and this whole school and everyone in it. Fuck the free and reduced lunch demographic, grubbing for spange, and smirking at me as I empty out my pockets. Fuck the cross country kids dirtying up the interior of my car cause their parents are too lazy to come pick them up from practice - get off your fucking ass and pretend you give a shit about your kids! Fuck the wannabe gangbangers strolling down the hallways with jeans around their knees, dirty ass finger nails and all sorts of product to "get dat monee" polluting my day. Inmates in fucking training. Fuck the adolescent males with deadbeat dads and teenage girls who give it up to any guy who can get it up. Going down on each other in my classrooms and on my stairwells, jingling their junk like the pimps and prostitutes on their party flyers. Fuck the repeat offenders with their ghetto ass slang and swag clothing with stickers still in tact. Proof of purchase my ass. 5 years since high school and you still haven't passed the graduation tests? Fuck the administrators and their political agendas. Power hungry children playing with walkie talkies, CCing and BCing to cover their own asses, mixing micromanagement and miscommunication so as never to provide a direct answer. Schemers with the final stamp of approval. Go back to the fucking classroom! I dare you. Fuck the well-intentioned fundraisers, going from one teacher to the next with their spirit wear and order forms. Selling me shit that I don't need! Fuck the board of education. Delusional masters of a world you know nothing about. Donald Trump, Celebrity Apprentice wannabe mother fuckers, figuring out new ways to rob hard working teachers of a balanced schedule. Send those hypocritical assholes to the Jersey Shore so they can get their asses beat by people who are just as dumb, deaf, and blind. You think I'm gonna believe your lies? Give me a fucking break! SACS! Furlough days! Fuck the thugnifican'ts. 20-inch wheels, in memory-of-stickers splattered all over their windshield, way to support your fucking family. And don't even get me started on the thugged out country boys, cuz they make the thugnfican'ts look swell. Fuck the Dade county natives, their misplaced pride, their gold teeth, showing off their area code tattoos, like their trying to audition for **Shottas**. Fuck the relocated New Yorkers with their ties to Brooklyn and their hip-hop declarations. Arrogant fucks with no drive or motivation, saying this schoolwork is boring. You're not fooling anybody, son! You can't read. Fuck the hurricane victims. Angry because their home was destroyed, they hate Georgia, and they'd rather take from someone instead of asking for help. And then they want to turn around and blame everything on the white man. Don't even know what slavery was and you wanna say, "Oh, that's racist," or "it's because I'm black." No, it's because you're fucking stupid, now let's move the fuck on! Fuck the rotating campus police officers with their inappropriate gestures and pepper spray, standing behind a guise of honor. Fuck the Fellowship of Christian Athletes. Fuck the special education teachers who put the real fucking degenerates in my classroom. Fuck the paperwork that protects them, delivering me into depression more times than I care to remember. And while you're at it, fuck all co-teachers everywhere. They get off way too easy. One day they're in class, they next day they're not, earning the same pay as other teachers when they don't teach shit. Fuck Osama Bin Laden, the War on Terror, and every fucking military recruiter who has come into my school. Fuck my principal. Narrow minded prick. Fuck my colleagues, making judgmental comments about the kids I teach. Fuck my students, I do everything I can to make class something to look forward to, and they still bitch, fucking unappreciative bastards. Fuck my endless guilt, sentencing myself to unneeded masochism, saying yes to nearly everything everyone asks of me, and all with a smile on my face. Fuck this whole school and everyone in it. From the English hall to the Magnet Building, from the Guidance Department to the Freshmen Academy. From the football clubhouse beside the track to the red brick band building to portable classrooms littering the outskirts of campus. Let a tornado rip it apart, let the floods swallow it whole, let it crumble to the fucking ground and then let the roaches revel in this desolate, life sucking space.

Neumann: Nawww...No. No, fuck you, Ryan Neumann. You had a choice, and this is what you chose, you dumb fuck.

When the mirror broke, my face shattered and fell to fragmented insignificance. I'm not sure who punched who. Might have been the reflection, but then again...

Sometimes I try to imagine my life as though it were a movie...as though I were a viewer watching some kind of story unfold. I often wonder if I would like what I see. Would I like the protagonist? Would I root for him? Would I be on his side?

Would I walk out of my own movie?

I drove home from school that night and knew something had to change.

I knew I had to make some kind of change.

Who was I becoming? That person in the bathroom?

Who the hell was that?

That night, while we were eating dinner, I told Mara I was not going to go back to my school for the impending school year. I told her I would apply for a transfer, or apply for teaching positions in other counties, but there was no way I was going back to that school for another year.

Doesn't your Principal have to approve your request? Mara asked.

Yeah, I think he does.

What if he...rejects it, or what if he doesn't approve it?

I'll quit.

That's the answer that worried her.

Sitting on the couch that night, and the many nights that followed, I began the process. I sent emails and resumes everywhere. Private schools, public schools, schools in other counties...it didn't matter. Anywhere was better than where I was. Initially, I hesitated on applying to other schools within my county because that required me to notify my Principal before sending even one resume to another high school within my county. He had to know I wanted to be somewhere else before I could be somewhere else. It was a momentary hesitation. I put on my most diplomatic disposition.

Good Afternoon Mr. Moline,

As the end of this school year is rapidly approaching, I have spent a great deal of time thinking about the upcoming 2011-2012 school year.

To be a bit more specific, the purpose of this email is to let you know first of all, that I have thoroughly enjoyed the past 5 years here. The second, and more pertinent, piece of this email is to let you know that I am interested in transferring to another high school for the 2011-2012 school year.

I will be completing the employee transfer information over the next few days, but wanted you to know what I have been thinking about, what my intentions are, and that while this has been an extremely difficult choice for me to make, wherever I end up next year, I intend to take the invaluable lessons I have learned here and represent this school in the best way that I can.

Sincerely,

Ryan Neumann

Later that day, Mr. Moline sent me another single statement reply.

Please come see me if you can today.

I did. It was the first time I had spoken to him since the whole Juno thing. That afternoon I found him in the student parking lot and as we walked back to his office, he told me he was surprised to hear that I was seeking a transfer. I was surprised to hear that he was surprised. He said I was at the top of a short list of teachers who they wanted for this Freshman Academy that would be opening next year. To my astonishment, he thought I was an innovative, out-of-the-box teacher who would be a perfect fit for this Academy. It was a chance for me to contribute to a program that had no box...something that I could truly help build.

Dumbfounded.

I was in shock. I told him that I was flattered, that I would have to chat with my wife about it, and that I truly appreciated his willingness to share that information with me. I had some thinking to do...and think I did.

The feelings of approval and vindication I felt that afternoon were temporary. They soon gave way to curiosity which in turn generated questions. Why am I only hearing about this now? Why was I unaware that Mr. Moline believed me to be a good teacher? Why should I care? Why do I care? I let the offer marinate for a day before emailing my decision.

Good Evening Mr. Moline ,

Once again, I just wanted to say thank you for taking the time to speak with me yesterday afternoon. I really appreciate everything you had to say...not to mention I was totally surprised to hear that I am one of the teachers you had in mind for the academy.

Over the past 24 hours, the Freshmen Academy has occupied nearly every thought I've had. Knowing that you see me as an innovative teacher, and believe that I would be a good fit for this brand new program has had a dramatic impact on where I see myself next school year. In fact, it's made this decision more difficult than I ever thought it could be.

With that being said, I would like to formally request that I be taken out of the teacher selection process for the Freshmen Academy. Although I have absolutely no idea where I will be teaching next year, I would like the opportunity to explore as many different avenues as possible. At the end of the day, that is what's driving, and what has driven, my decision. I would like to experience as many different walks of life as I can, and the idea of not knowing where I will be next year has made that desire more and more appealing.

I wish you and everyone else involved with the Freshmen Academy all the best.

Sincerely,

Ryan Neumann

New beginnings...I'm not sure we get many...not sure if we are privy to an overwhelming amount of opportunities which allow us to reinvent ourselves...to start over and begin again. And if so, if, when they arrive, are we aware of these moments in life? I wonder about that.

Sometimes...yeah, sometimes I think we are aware.

So ummmm, what the hell.

It's not so much a question as it is an overall observation.

My life as a teacher.

What (*pause*) the (*longer pause*) hell?

That's what I'd been asking myself every single school day for the past 5 years. What the hell am I doing? What the hell am I supposed to be doing? What the hell am I teaching? Hell...am I teaching?

What the hell am I doing with my life?

I have now learned the answers to some of these questions. That last one though, the one about life, guess we'll just have to wait and see what happens.

Not so very long ago, I sent a query to the high school I was once a student at. Inquiring about the nature of future positions, I expressed an interest in coming home. I said I would very much appreciate the opportunity to teach where I was taught.

Funny how things work out. Looking back on it now, it's almost as if my old high school was waiting for me to apply. It's been ten years since I graduated from high school, and next year I will be teaching in a classroom where I was once a student.

Next year I will no longer be an english teacher.

I will work, learn, and strive to be an English teacher.

In the time that has elapsed since then, since the roles have been reversed, since I have chosen to embark on this journey in the realm of education, I can tell you that if I have learned nothing else, I have learned how to respond to one question...or maybe not so much a question as it is an overall observation on life. However, this response requires me to do something my parents told me to never do; answer a question with a question. But when faced with predicaments that are tied so closely to meanings of life and death and perhaps even truth ...or when asked if you ever thought you would do this or that, or to even consider this or that, I can think of only one plausible reply.

What the hell, why not?

I've heard teachers and non-teachers alike say,

Those who can...do.

Those who cannot...teach.

But what about those who cannot teach?

Well, in my case, they transfer to another school and write about what had happened.

ABOUT A NEUMANN

Ryan Lund Neumann graduated from Pope High School in 2001. Located in Cobb County, Georgia, Neumann would have adamantly disputed any desire to become a teacher upon his graduation from the previously mentioned high school should you have asked him at that point in his life...not that you would have. From 2001 to 2004, Neumann attended Appalachian State University in Boone, North Carolina where he majored in English, specifically Creative Writing, and minored in Special Education. After that, it was onward to the University of Georgia for Neumann. He studied diligently and with great determination managed to win the heart of a young woman (Mara) whom he had been infatuated with since his junior year of high school. Oh, and in 2006 he also earned a Masters degree in Secondary English Education. The 5 years following led to the creating, writing, and publishing of **What Had Happened.**   From 2006 to 2011, Neumann taught high school english at South Cobb High School...also located in Cobb County, Georgia. Now if you've gotten to this part of the book, Neumann will stop referring to himself in the third person and say, I hope that after my writing this book, and you reading this book, I am still allowed to teach where I was taught.

13156906R00130

Made in the USA
Lexington, KY
20 January 2012